Crystals for Beginners

A Beginners Guide to Heal Yourself Through the Hidden Power of Crystals

Emily Oddo

Contents

Introduction

A magnificent citrine cluster.
"You know the world is a magical place when Mother Earth grows her own jewelry."

Inspiring Quotes, 2022

Crystals have fascinated mankind since the beginning of time. They were held in high esteem, not only for their beauty, but also for the magical powers the ancient civilizations ascribed to them.

What if all the ancient knowledge and more could be at your fingertips? What if you could learn to use the right crystals and gemstones to lead the happiest, healthiest, and most fulfilled life possible for you?

It is not a fairy tale! I'm going to tell you how in this book you're reading now. Crystals are powerful instruments that can be used to great advantage for ourselves and others.

However, finding your way through the maze of information available online and elsewhere is not easy. There is a bewildering variety of crystals in existence, and to each one, specific attributes are ascribed. Crystal experts, unfortunately, don't always agree on these attributes and it can become confusing to a novice in the field.

I know what that feels like, having been down the same road myself. I read everything I could find, talked to anyone who would answer my questions, and ended up in such a tangle that I almost gave up.

However, I persevered, and this book is the result. You can now take a shortcut through the confusion by simply reading the treasure trove of information in *Crystals for Beginners*. You will hit the ground running and be ready to implement your new knowledge immediately.

The emphasis in the book is on practical explanations and tips, rather than the theoretical side of why crystals work. Crystals are amazing but applying their power to benefit us is more important.

After a short introduction on each stone, you will learn how to recognize each one, as well as the color varieties available and their important traits. We'll look at their areas of healing and balancing and discuss how each crystal and stone should be used for the best results. Lastly, you will learn how to clean and treat your crystals to keep them at their best and make sure they don't sustain any damage.

Are you ready? Fasten your seatbelt and get ready to start your awesome healing journey with crystals!

A Word of Caution, Though...

Since the start of the Covid-19 pandemic, general interest in crystals has peaked. While it was once thought to be the domain of millennials and members of Gen Z, it has now become more mainstream than ever before.

The need to calm Covid-19-induced anxiety and restore clear thinking has sent crystal buying through the roof, according to an article on bloomberg.com. Many people also developed an emotional need to give meaningful gifts to their loved ones; with near-gemstones in a lower price bracket than diamonds and other precious stones, the crystal market entered a billion-dollar-phase (Elliott, 2020).

The downside of the market boom is that unscrupulous dealers also saw an opportunity to make a fast buck. Please make sure you buy from a reputable shop—I don't want you to waste your money and become disillusioned because you purchased a stone of low quality (or even a fake) without knowing it. Buying online, if you're a beginner, can be especially risky.

Another important point to keep in mind is that some crystals are sourced from poor countries where the miners and their families are paid little for their work. Some mines even operate in conditions that are unfavorable toward the workers.

Let's do our part to look after the well-being of all the world's people. Find out where the gems you want to buy come from and what their history is. That will help ensure that we don't support inhumane or cruel mining operations.

A Health Disclaimer

The tips in this book are not intended to take the place of your medical practitioner's advice. If you have any serious ailments, do not put off going to the doctor or ignore their opinion.

Instead, use your crystals as supplementary benefits to strengthen any medication you might be taking.

Chapter 1

The Basics of Crystal Healing

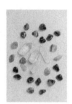

Assorted crystals and gemstones.

"In a crystal we have clear evidence of the existence of a formative life principle, and though we cannot understand the life of a crystal, it is nonetheless a living being."

Nikola Tesla, Inspiring Quotes, 2022

How Are Crystals Formed?

A crystal forms whenever a liquid body solidifies. It can be a chemical element, a compound, or a mixture. The solidification forms in a regular internal pattern.

Crystals usually start small, but as more atoms join the formation, they grow organically.

They vary greatly in color and texture. Some are hard as rocks, while others are soft and porous.

The grid-like crystalline pattern occurs in many places in nature—think of salt and sugar, for instance, or the brilliant ice crystals inside snowflakes.

There are seven basic patterns: cubic, trigonal, tetragonal, monoclinic, triclinic, orthorhombic, and hexagonal. The pattern does not influence the external shape of the crystal, only the internal pattern or lattice.

The Birth of a Crystal

As with all births, the formation of a crystal is also an awe-inspiring event. Most crystals are formed underground, when liquid rock, known as magma, cools. Crystals can also form in water or even from fumes.

The environment where the cooling and hardening happen, the amount of space available to grow, the pressure, the temperature, and the chemical composition of the source material determine the shape, color, and lattice of the crystal.

The process takes place over many years. Sometimes it gets interrupted by movements in the earth's crust, resuming when the growth channel opens again with the next shift of the tectonic plates. The process of stop-and-start growth leaves a mark on the crystals. There are often color variations within one crystal, or different formations growing on a base. This can produce spectacular crystals. I'm sure once you've seen a multi-colored stone, like a watermelon tourmaline, you'll understand!

- You might find it interesting to know that the earth's crust is about three miles thick under the seabed and 25 miles deep under the continents. Under the crust is the liquid and fiery mantle that makes up 83% of the earth's volume—it is close to 2,000 miles thick! The bottom of the crust is full of crannies and small craters from the interaction with the superhot magma in the mantle. These provide ideal locations for crystals to grow.

- If magma reaches the surface through a volcanic eruption, it is called lava (Clark, 2015).

Sometimes two different source materials start growing at the same time, but they crystallize at different speeds. The slower one will end up being engulfed by the faster one. An example of this is Colombian emeralds that grow with pieces of pyrite inside. This combination brings interesting qualities to the stone when it is used in healing.

Various impurities can also become embedded in a crystal, such as rutile encased inside a quartz crystal.

The inclusions in emeralds are usually too small to see with the naked eye.

Scientific Studies

Although many studies have been done on crystallography and mineralogy, not much has happened scientifically regarding the healing powers of crystals.

An 1880 study conducted by brothers Jack and Pierre Curie discovered that it is possible to produce electricity by changing the temperature of crystals and putting pressure on them. The pressure causes ions in the crystal to shift. That disturbs the internal balance which, in turn, transforms the crystal into a tiny battery.

Their finding is now known as the piezoelectric effect. It has helped our modern technology greatly and is commonly found in equipment such as inkjet printers, microphones, sonar, and quartz watches (Rekstis, 2022).

The piezoelectric effect suggests that touching a crystal can influence the body's energy levels and vibrational frequency.

In the electronics industry, quartz crystals are mainly used as resonators. That means they synchronize and equalize the electric energy created in components of electrical circuits, such as oscillators (Grigalunas, 2019).

Their job is to synchronize and "even out" electrical charges —exactly what you and I need in our minds and bodies when we become diseased and uncomfortable.

Modern scientists have so far ascribed any reports of healing to the placebo effect, but even if that is the only way crystals work for us, it is still a valid outcome.

In a study done on distant healing intervention in seriously ill patients, Dr. Marilyn Schlitz found clear evidence that spiritual healing and prayer created positive physical changes (Schlitz, 2005).

Healing With Crystals

Every crystal has its own vibrational frequency that comes from the material from which it was formed. They are alive with energy—the very substance of life.

I remember touching my first crystal. It was a magical experience that shot warm tingles through my hand and arm. Moving my hand from one crystal to another, it was easy to feel strong energy from some and weaker energy from others. That was because, usually, the crystal that 'speaks' to you is the one you need.

Let's go into the vibrations in more detail.

Getting the Vibrations

A crystal can be described as a vault of power. It holds within itself all the energy peculiar to its nature. When that stone is placed anywhere on the body or kept in the body's vicinity, the power is transmitted through the vibrational frequencies that emanate from the crystal. The molecular interaction arising from the crystal's composition creates the vibrations.

The vibrations enhance our bodies' ability to heal while acting like a magnet to draw out negative energy.

Do I perhaps hear you say now, "Hold on a minute, how can vibrations work with my body?"

Let's back up a bit for a brief and simple physics explanation.

Everything in the universe vibrates. Even the things that appear stationary to us are constantly resonating, oscillating, and moving at various frequencies. Frequencies measure the number of times an event occurs within a known time period. When we're talking about the vibration of molecules, the frequency denotes the number of cycles a particle completes per second (Hunt, 2018).

Resonance is an essential part of this explanation and central to how crystal healing works. When two moving objects come into proximity to each other, they tend to synchronize their movements. In other words, they start vibrating at the same tempo.

This tendency is also known as spontaneous self-organization. It lies at the heart of, among other things, our responses to external stimuli. It is also the way the neurons in our bodies communicate with each other so that we can function smoothly.

When we get sick or suffer mental discomfort, the diseased part of our bodies no longer vibrates at the right frequency to stay healthy. The right crystal on or close to the problem site can bring resonant vibration to the body of the person being treated, to restore the 'healthy' frequency.

Accessing the Earth's Healing Power

You might have seen references to crystals as "record keepers." This is because they hold a whole history of the earth with her elements and energy inside them. The lattice of the stone contains a chemically pure record of the mineral from which it was formed, thereby emitting a clear, strong energy signature. When we use crystals, we access this powerful energetic history to balance, ground, cleanse, and heal us.

Their ability to ground us is especially helpful when trying to make sense of disasters, such as wars and natural crises like the Covid-19 pandemic.

Besides the general benefit, the energy vibrations also correspond to specific areas in our bodies. More on that a little later.

How Do Crystals Help Us?

Crystals are true holistic healers. They work on the spiritual, physical, emotional, and mental levels of our being.

As electromagnetic creatures, our systems can go out of balance and create discomfort and disease. Once balance is restored, we are free to function optimally again.

Ailments and mental issues can be caused by several factors, including disconnection between vital systems, worries about physical circumstances, feeling unsupported or unloved, general anxiety, and an inability to trust the universe. Crystals can gently address all your problems and lead you to a life of calm connectedness to whatever you perceive as the source of all life and abundance.

Where Do I Start?

Before you rush out to buy a bagful of crystals, it is important to identify what you need them for.

Take a few minutes and make a list of what you want to heal or accomplish. Do you have physical ailments? Do you have mental and/or emotional issues? Or do you only want a protective stone, maybe?

Your goals will determine the stones you will buy.

If there are any other crystals that speak to you strongly, almost pulling you toward them, consider purchasing them. You might know intuitively that you need their energy.

Which Form Is More Effective?

Crystals are sold in many different forms, from raw beauties to fine jewelry and everything in between.

Again, it's best to follow your gut about what will be the most effective to accomplish your goals.

Crystal home decorations such as eggs or coasters work well if you want a specific stone's energy in your vicinity without the crystal touching your body or to cleanse a room.

A new trend is water bottles with a "gem pod" in the bottom to energize the water.

You can also purchase crystal sex toys to enhance your sexual energy.

For crystals that touch the skin, there is a huge variety of jewelry available. From rings and bracelets to necklaces and earrings, there is something to suit every taste.

An alternative to jewelry is prayer beads that can be worn around the wrist or next to the heart.

Follow your intuition when making your choice. Remember that the ones that call to you are the ones to choose.

Crystal Shapes

Crystals come in numerous different shapes and sizes; some have sharp points while others are rounded. Some are in clusters and others stand alone. Some are pillars and others are balls. Many crystals are also artificially cut into specific forms.

Each of these shapes have their own significance and will influence the results you get from working with your crystals.

Don't despair in confusion though, as we'll unpack all the benefits of the different shapes in the next section.

Points

Pointed crystals are used two ways in healing. When the crystal is pointed away from the body, it draws negative energy away.

When the crystal is pointed toward the body, it channels positive energy toward the person receiving the healing.

Double Termination

Some crystals have two points—one at the top end and one

at the bottom. That means that the crystal's energy is simultaneously radiated or absorbed from both ends.

It is used to achieve balance between spirit and matter, providing a bridge between the energies.

It is believed that placing a double-terminated crystal on the third eye can enhance telepathic abilities (Hall, 2009).

Clusters

A cluster is a collection of many crystals, pointing in many different directions.

They are extensively used to clear a room or other crystals because they radiate energy to the surrounding environment.

Geodes

Geodes are crystals enclosed within an outer shell. There is a cave-like opening in the middle.

The crystals point toward the middle, so geodes are excellent for diffusing and softening harsh energies. They retain their positive energy in the hollow center and release it slowly.

They are used for protection and spiritual growth.

Natural Wands

These are long, straight, and pointed crystals. They are found in all healers' toolkits because they transfer healing energy rapidly down their straight line.

Balls

Balls emit energy in all directions at the same time and are therefore deemed to be windows into time.

They are usually used in a practice known as scrying to discern events in the future or the past.

Squares

Squares are excellent for grounding because they consolidate energy within themselves.

Some crystals, such as fluorite, occur naturally in a square form.

Pyramids

If you want to focus energy, a pyramid is your go-to shape. They amplify their vibrations between the four sides and send tightly focused energy out through the apex.

They are especially useful in chakra work.

Eggs

Egg-shaped crystals are used to detect energy blockages and clear them easily.

The more pointed end can be used for massage or acupuncture, while the entire object fits comfortably in the hand for stress release.

Layers

These crystals look like several plates stacked on top of each other. That enables them to work at many energy levels at the same time.

This trait can be useful when you must get to the bottom of an issue.

The Key Takeaways

- Crystals form in various substances when liquid cools and hardens.
- The source substance provides the characteristics of the crystal.
- Crystals are widely used in modern technology as resonators to equalize energy levels.
- Healing with crystals produces the same equalizing effect in our bodies.
- When purchasing crystals, choose a reputable dealer and look for stones that are ethically produced.
- Choose your crystals to suit your needs, both in shape and form.

Are you ready to start working with your crystals? In the next chapter, we'll explore how to clean, charge, and care for your precious energy stones.

Chapter 2

Cleaning, Charging, and Caring for Your Crystals

"If you want to find the secrets of the universe, think in terms of energy, frequency, and vibration."

Nikola Tesla, My Tunbridge Wells, 2021

Crystals need some looking after to remain at their best vibrations. They must also be cleaned and charged before the first use to sensitize them to your needs.

Charging a New Crystal

Your new crystal friend must get to know you. Your energy must initiate a dance with the crystal's energy for it to affect you positively. If this interaction is not activated, you could spend a lifetime sharing your space with crystals and not receiving anything from them.

Your intention is important when working with your crystals. Just like with any relationship, a grateful and appreciative energy coming from one side will be reciprocated from the other side.

Your crystal traveled a long distance before ending up in your home. It was handled by many hands, and it absorbed all the energies it picked up on the journey. It is likely that a fair share of these energies were negative or simply not in line with your own. Before you can impress your own energetic signature upon your crystal, you must clean the accumulated 'other' energies from it.

Cleaning and Charging Your Crystals

The cleaning and charging take place in the same step. Although one product or medium is used, two different aims are accomplished.

To understand this better, you can compare it with your skin care routine. The cleaning part removes the makeup and sweat of the day, while the serum you pat on before getting into bed recharges your skin to its full beauty.

You will need to do this before the first use of your crystal, as well as periodically afterward. When it seems like your crystal has lost its potency, it is time for another cleaning and recharging session.

There are several ways to clean and charge a crystal. Just make sure that the crystal you want to work with can tolerate the method you choose. Some can't be submerged in water, for instance.

.   .   .

Water

For any hard stone, such as amethyst, quartz, or moonstone, holding it for a minute at a time under running water from the faucet or submerging it in flowing natural water, like a river, are the quickest cleaning methods. You can move your fingers all over the stone to wash away the negative energies and, at the same time, start imprinting the stone with your own energy.

If you're unsure whether your crystal can be submerged, a general rule-of-thumb is that stones with names ending in "-ite" are brittle and/or soft and can't tolerate water.

Pat the stone dry with a soft cloth after washing it.

Salt

Hard stones can be buried under rock or Himalayan salt for up to 48 hours. Softer stones, such as turquoise and opal, scratch easily, so salt is not a good cleaning method for them.

If you don't have enough salt to completely bury your stones, you can dissolve a teaspoon of salt in a bowl of water. (Table salt will also work if you don't have rock or Himalayan salt on hand.) If you're lucky enough to live near the ocean, you can use sea water. If they can be put in water, submerge the stones completely.

For the first time cleaning and charging, the stone should be left overnight in the salt or salt solution. For maintenance, one hour should be enough.

Remove the stones from the salt water when the time is up and pat them dry.

Brown Rice

Burying your stones completely in a bowl of brown rice is a method that is safe for any type of crystal or stone.

Leave them there for 24 hours before discarding all the rice.

Saging (Smudging)

Any type of stone can be cleaned with sage. Burning sage leaves and cleaning a space or object with the smoke is called smudging. It is a sacred ritual to some people.

You'll need some loose or bundled sage and a fire-safe bowl to burn the leaves in. Make sure you open a window or do your smudging outside.

Light the tip of the sage and hold the smoking plant material in your non-dominant hand. Take the stone with your dominant hand and move it through the smoke.

Hold each stone in the smoke for 30 to 60 seconds.

Natural Light

The light of both the moon and the sun are great for cleaning and charging hard crystals. Put them directly on the ground, if possible, to amplify the effects of the light with the vibrations of the earth.

You can put your stone out in the moonlight by nightfall

and bring it in again the next day before eleven o'clock. That will ensure the stone gets the energy of the moon *and* sun, but it must be brought into shade before the sun gets so hot that it cracks or discolors the crystal.

However, I would not use direct sunlight on vibrantly colored stones, such as amethyst.

Soil

Burying a stone in soil can clean and recharge a crystal well. Just make sure the stone you're burying is not so soft that the soil particles can scratch it.

If you have a small earthenware pot or jar, you can fill that with soil and bury the stone within it.

How long you keep the stone buried is up to you but give it at least a week. If you take it out and the energy emanating from it still feels sluggish or heavy, you can rebury it until the crystal feels light again.

Sound

Sound is a powerful use of vibrations. You can give your crystal a sound bath by immersing it in one pitch or tone for five to ten minutes.

The specific pitch does not matter too much if the sound is loud and sustained enough to penetrate the crystal and vibrate its particles.

The sound can be achieved by using a tuning fork, singing bowl, bell, or chanting a mantra. I received excellent results when I put one crystal at a time into a singing bowl and then played the bowl. A note of caution on this, though: the vibrations of the singing bowl can cause the crystals to bump around slightly. Soft stones could get damaged this way, especially if you put more than one into the bowl.

If you have an extended collection of stones to cleanse and charge, a sound bath is a practical way to reach them all.

- Tuning forks are made in set frequencies. If you want to use a specific frequency, consider a dedicated crystal tuner. These tuners resonate at 4,096 Hz, which is believed to be the vibrating frequency of quartz as well as of the earth.

Clusters

Large crystal clusters are not only pretty, but they can also be used to clean and charge smaller stones.

Place the small stone in the middle or on top of the cluster for at least 24 hours.

Amethyst geodes and selenite slabs will work equally well.

Cleaner Stones

Carnelian, hematite, and clear quartz are said to be cleaners of other stones.

Crystals of these three are usually smaller in size, so you might need several.

Cover the bottom of a bowl with the smaller stones and put the crystal to be cleaned on top of them. Let them sit for at least 24 hours.

Breath

You can use your breath, combined with your pure intentions, to cleanse and recharge your crystals.

Empty your mind of everything except the intention you want to hold for the crystal. Then inhale deeply while holding the crystal in one hand. Exhale forcefully over the crystal while waving your other hand over it.

Keep this up for about 30 seconds.

Spirit Guides

If you have a spirit guide, you can ask them to make a connection between you and the stone and communicate your energy and intention that way.

Visualizations

Hold the crystal in your hands and quiet your mind. Visualize a pure, bright light forming between your hands, enveloping the crystal.

See the radiant light swirling around the stone, moving and lifting all the negative energies trapped inside it.

As the negativity disappears from the crystal, the light gets brighter until the stone itself seems to shine.

When you feel an openness and freshness from the stone, you can stop the visualization.

Build Yourself a Charging Station

A little charging station makes it easy to charge smaller crystals while also being a focal point in your decor.

Get yourself a small, inexpensive glass terrarium like those being sold on Amazon. Cover the bottom with rock or pink Himalayan salt and put it near a window where the natural light can bathe the crystals inside. Hold your hands over the terrarium and send your intention to it, carried on a bright light, before using it the first time.

Simply put the crystals to be charged on the bed of salt and leave them overnight.

* * *

Make Them Part of Your Routine

Your crystals can be used in your space and/or on your body. The more you are in close contact with your crystal, the stronger its effect will be on you.

With our hectic schedules, we don't always have time for daily quiet conversations with our crystals. Your second-best option remains carrying a crystal in your pocket or even in your bra to experience its helpful and calming effects when you need them most.

Let's look at some specific ways to incorporate crystals into your daily routine.

Wear Them as Jewelry

There is such a huge variety of crystal jewelry to choose from that every taste should be able to find something.

Both men and women can wear bracelets, rings, and neck chains. Full necklaces and ear ornaments might be more popular with the girls, although there is no reason why a man can't wear them too.

If you choose a piece of jewelry that gets worn against your skin 24/7, just make sure that the stone can withstand skin oils and sweat.

Use Them as Home Décor

Crystals are not only pretty to look at, but they can also fill your living space with balance and love, banishing negativity and bringing ease into the hearts of the residents.

Although somewhat on the expensive side, one big crystal or cluster makes an excellent focal point as a decoration. You can also opt for a variety of smaller crystals, scattered throughout your space or gathered in collections.

Add Them to Your Home Altar

A home altar is a dedicated space in your home for conveying your intentions to the cosmos. Adding crystals to the items you already have there can strengthen the energy you want to accompany your intentions.

Try writing down any specific intentions and placing a crystal on the paper. The results might surprise you.

Bring Their Energy Into Your Yoga and Meditation Practices

Placing crystals all around you while doing yoga or holding a crystal while meditating will fill you with positive, calm energy.

They can help you open to the spiritual world and enter higher realms of consciousness, bringing with it deep peace.

Hold Them on Your Body

To balance, open, or heal a specific organ or chakra, you can hold a crystal right on the spot where it is needed while sending healing light and love.

You can also place an appropriate crystal on your third eye while meditating.

In a later chapter, we'll discuss the chakras and their associated stones in detail.

Make A Sacred Geometrical Grid

The idea behind sacred geometry is that using the patterns can give the energy behind an intention a serious boost.

There are several patterns, such as a medicine wheel,

infinity loop, spiral, or labyrinth. A quick Google search will give you printable patterns to make it easier. Choose a pattern that speaks to you.

Choose the stones that will enhance your intention. If you want to manifest abundance, for example, you could go for a grid containing jade, amber, citrine, and green aventurine.

Start laying your crystals down from the outside in while keeping your intention at the front of your mind. The last crystal, known as the master crystal, goes in the middle.

Spend a few minutes dedicating the grid to be used in the manifestation of your intention.

Take Them to Work

Keeping a colorful crystal on your desk is not just lovely to look at, but it can also help you stay focused on your work. They promote mental sharpness and can also enhance your creativity.

Are you headed into a meeting with someone who always gets your hackles up? Take the right stone with you in your pocket. It will help you keep your cool.

Welcome Them to Your Selfcare Routine

Crystal face rollers in different styles and a gua sha stone.

From taking a bath with your favorite crystal (if it can withstand water) to making crystals part of your skincare, they can help you put your best foot forward.

A gentle face massage with a crystal roller will infuse your skin with a healthy glow while promoting cell rejuvenation. Put a neutral oil, such as coconut, on the roller before use to help it glide smoothly over your skin.

You can also incorporate a gua sha stone. Gua sha originated in the ancient Chinese dynasties, where it was the preferred method of skin stimulation for elite Chinese ladies. The curve of the stone is designed to fit the contours of the face. A gentle scraping activates pressure points to reduce stress and stimulate lymphatic drainage to eliminate excess fluid. Goodbye puffy face!

Say Goodnight to Your Crystals

Soothe away the stress of the day and fall asleep with your mind at peace. Place some crystals in your bedroom and use a crystal light.

You can work out a calming bedtime routine, such as sitting quietly with a cup of herbal tea and some relaxing crystals in your lap before you get into bed. You could also turn this time into a short meditation for emotional balance and tranquility.

Remember to switch off all your electronic equipment before doing this; you don't want their blue light or electromagnetic frequencies interfering with your rest.

Create Crystal Essences

For thousands of years, healers and beauticians have made essences of crystals to drink, use on the skin, add to a bath, or refresh a room.

Although the ancient technique involved crushing the stones, you don't need to destroy your precious crystals to get the benefits. You can simply soak your chosen crystals in water or a carrier oil. Remember to use stones that can tolerate water or oil.

The general rule is that a water base is for drinking, while an oil base is for topical use. Some crystals, unfortunately, have toxic properties, so do your research before you choose your stones.

Clean the stones first, so you don't end up with debris in your essences.

You can combine two different stones in one liquid, but not more than two. You don't want them canceling out each other's healing effects.

Sterilize a glass container and fill it with about 16 ounces of water or carrier oil, such as jojoba, coconut, or grape seed.

Using a wooden spoon, gently lower your crystals into the liquid while setting your intention for the essence.

Place the container in a spot where sunlight or moonlight will shine on it directly. You will need at least seven hours for water-based essences and 24 hours for oil-based ones.

Remove the crystals with your wooden spoon when the time is up and fill your spray bottle or other appropriate vessel for the intended uses.

Unused essences can be stored in the refrigerator for a few days. Oil-based liquids will last longer than water-based essences.

Caring for Your Crystals

Some crystals are fragile and can break or scratch easily. Only tumbled stones have tough, smooth surfaces, acquired after hours of being tumbled in fine grit.

Keep your stones wrapped individually in a silk or velvet

cloth when they are not in use and store them in a cool, dry place. Tumbled stones can be kept together in a soft bag.

Take special care with crystals that are layered or clustered, as they can separate when handled roughly.

The Key Takeaways

- A new crystal must be cleansed from the negative energy it picked up on its journey to you and charged with your own energy.
- There are several ways to do this, and it is important to know what your crystal can tolerate.
- Once they're charged, your crystals can become an integral part of your daily routine.
- It is important to know the characteristics of your crystals to care for them properly.

Let's dive now into the next chapter, which is all about the top, must-have crystals.

Chapter 3

Top 10 Crystals You Need to Have

"If my life was a reference book, it would be filled with wisdom, humor, and very colorful crystals."

Anonymous, 2022

How much would you be willing to pay for a new drug that claims to heal all your physical and mental ailments? I bet you would try your best to find the money for it, without asking too many questions.

Crystals can do the same for you, but at a fraction of the cost and with no harmful side effects. That sounds like a win-win situation to me!

Although there are different opinions on exactly which crystals are essential, there are 10 that all the experts agree on. They cover all the areas that we, as humans, are likely to need some help with.

The energy of these stones is also strong enough that it doesn't matter if you can only afford a small crystal, as it will still be effective.

As a bonus, all of them are gorgeous to look at too.

Rose Quartz

A beautiful raw piece of rose quartz.

At the top of the list for love, acceptance, and compassion is rose quartz. It works for all relationships to bring peace and harmony.

The earth has perhaps never needed our compassion and love more than it does right now with global warming, natural disasters, and the Covid-19 pandemic. We can turn the tide by making it a priority to work with our rose quartz crystals on this essential relationship.

Appearance

Rose quartz is a pink stone, ranging from pale, whitish pink to medium dark pink, and is usually translucent.

Rarity

It is not rare at all. Rose quartz can be found in abundance in Brazil, India, South Africa, Japan, Madagascar, and the US.

Uses

Rose quartz is often called the stone of love. It is associated with unconditional love and deep peace. If you have a relationship in your life that needs repairing or you are looking for true love, this stone is the one to use.

It gently draws negative energy away from you and your situation and replaces it with the good vibrations of trust and harmony.

It also enhances empathy and sensitivity for others' feelings.

Are you facing a big change in your life that you struggle to accept, such as menopause, divorce, or getting retrenched? Rose quartz can help with that too. If you set your intention to be positive and kind to yourself, the stone will amplify your loving mindset.

Releasing unhealed emotional trauma and heartache can be

almost as bad as experiencing the feelings the first time. Use rose quartz to soothe the process, comfort your grief, and start the healing journey.

This stone can also play a vital role in learning to forgive and accept yourself unconditionally.

Physically speaking, rose quartz is used to strengthen the heart and blood circulation. It also aids in the release of impurities from all the body fluids. When used on the thymus, it can help to strengthen the lungs.

Many people also believe rose quartz increases fertility because it opens the heart and mind to all kinds of love.

Position

A rose quartz crystal can be worn over the heart or thymus. Alternatively, it can be placed in a space, such as the bedroom, where love is needed or feng shui-style in the relationship corner of your house.

Associated Zodiac Sign and Element

Rose quartz is associated with Taurus, which is an Earth element sign.

Moonstone

A circular grid of moonstones.

Moonstone is said to denote new beginnings. It is strongly connected to intuition and the feminine energy of the moon.

It serves as a gentle reminder that everything comes and goes in cycles, just like the moon waxes and wanes. That can put us in a reflective frame of mind that calms stormy emotions and allows the deep inner knowledge of our souls to come to our conscious attention.

Appearance

Moonstones can be found in either white, yellow, cream, green, or blue. They have a milky appearance, and all sides are translucent.

. . .

Rarity

They are not scarce and can be collected in Sri Lanka, Australia, and India.

Uses

Because moonstone is so intimately connected to intuition, it can open the mind to psychic abilities and synchronicities. A moonstone pendant has traditionally been worn to develop abilities, such as clairvoyance.

It reduces stress and soothes emotional upsets. When worn on the solar plexus, it can help to recognize and release old emotional patterns that don't serve you anymore, replacing them with emotionally intelligent new pathways.

Moonstone has a powerful connection to the female reproductive system. It can heal hormone imbalances, reduce hormonal fluid retention, and reset the biorhythmic clock.

Your digestive system will also appreciate some aid from a couple of moonstones to shake off sluggishness and eliminate toxins.

Position

Commercially available moonstones tend to be small, so they work well in jewelry pieces such as rings and pendants.

Alternatively, the stone can be placed on the appropriate body part, such as the forehead for spiritual awakening, the solar plexus for emotional patterns, or the heart to calm dramatic emotions.

. . .

Associated Zodiac Sign and Element
Moonstone is associated with Cancer, which is a Water element sign.

* * *

Amethyst

Amethyst crystals in their natural state, as part of a geode.

The splendid purple beauty of an amethyst is valued the world over. Once thought to be only worthy of royalty, the stones are now often used as decorations and healing aids.

Appearance
Amethysts can appear in every different hue of purple you can think of, from the palest lilac to deep, rich aubergine. They are transparent, pointed crystals and often appear in clusters or geodes.

They don't do well in prolonged direct sunlight and the color will fade after a while.

Rarity

They are one of the most common stones in the world and can be found in Britain, Canada, East Africa, Siberia, the US, India, Russia, Mexico, Brazil, Sri Lanka, and Uruguay.

The huge basalt cavities in Uruguay and Brazil contain several tons of crystals.

Uses

Amethysts relate to spiritual enlightenment. They are credited with having extremely powerful protective powers that vibrate at a high frequency.

It is used to block negative environmental influences and enhance spiritual awareness, making it a strong ally in meditation. It helps to focus the mind and think clearly.

If you feel scattered and pulled between the highs and lows in your life, call on an amethyst to balance and center you again. It alleviates grief and dispels anger and fear.

You might have heard amethyst being called the stone of sobriety. That epithet came from the stone's calming effect on overindulgence and uncontrolled physical passions.

Amethysts are used for scrying and general stimulation of the third eye.

Physically, amethysts are thought to boost hormones and

finetune the metabolism. The stone assists with clearing out toxins and strengthens the immune system.

It can ease headaches, as well as reduce swelling and bruising.

Position

Clusters and geodes are effective as space purifiers, while single points are used in healing. When the point faces toward you, it will draw energy to you. Points facing outward will pull energy away from you.

A single crystal can be worn over the heart or throat or placed on the third eye during meditation.

If your sleep is troubled by nightmares, you can put an amethyst under your pillow.

Associated Zodiac Sign and Element

Amethyst is associated with Pisces, which is a Water element sign.

Clear Quartz

Clear quartz crystals in a natural formation.

Clear quartz, or rock crystal, as it's sometimes called, is known as the master stone because of its wide range of healing properties and applications. Its crystal structure is a helical spiral that is unique among crystals.

Appearance

They are found in long, pointed, clear crystals. They are transparent but can be striated or milky. They often form big clusters.

.   .   .

Rarity

Clear quartz is found worldwide and is easily obtainable.

Uses

Quartz can be used to heal and balance any condition and in any healing modality. It is, for instance, believed that coating acupuncture needles in quartz increases their effectiveness by 10 percent (Hall, 2009).

The crystal's vibrations attune themselves to the person needing the healing and attune them to the perfect state for the disease to be healed.

It acts as a powerful cleanser on all spiritual levels and can dissolve negative karmic seeds.

Because it acts as a spiritual record keeper, it can help us unlock our memories and focus our concentration.

Position

A clear quartz crystal can be placed or worn wherever it is needed.

Associated Zodiac Sign and Element

Clear quartz is associated with Aries and Leo, which are both Fire element signs.

Black Tourmaline

Black tourmaline in its raw form.

Black tourmaline is one of nature's best cleaners, making quick work of transforming heavy energy to lighter, higher vibrations. This makes it a valuable chakra stone because it can balance all the chakras.

In ancient times, magicians used black tourmaline as protection against earth demons when they were casting spells.

Appearance

Tourmaline is found in various colors, but black is the most used stone. It is an opaque, striated silicate crystal, also known as Schorl.

Its plentiful ridges and furrows are cool to the touch. When polished, the stone is a brilliantly shining jet black.

Rarity

Although it is found in several countries, it is often not

easily obtainable in shops. However, most specialist stores will stock it.

Uses

The pitch black of this mysterious-looking stone is believed to swallow all negative energy and protect the wearer against any spiritual attacks. Shamans often incorporate it in their rituals.

Black tourmaline can provide some protection against electromagnetic waves and radiation.

Natural wands are used to clear the aura and bring back objectivity to troubled situations. It relieves tension and the wearer of the crystal will be able to think positively again and find solutions to problems.

In gardens, black tourmaline acts as a natural deterrent to insects and aids the healthy growth of all plants when buried in the soil.

Using this stone in meditation, it is possible to journey deep into yourself, banish all fears, and replace them with compassion and inspiration.

The stone can balance the right and left-brain hemispheres to enhance creativity and boost a positive mental attitude.

Position

It can be placed or worn where needed. To ward off unwanted electromagnetic energy, it should be placed between you and the object emitting the frequencies with the point away from you.

A gem essence of black tourmaline is also effective.

Associated Zodiac Sign and Element

Black tourmaline is associated with Libra and Scorpio. Libra is an Air element sign and Scorpio is a Water element sign.

Jade

A jade figurine of a bear in an amethyst geode.

Appearance

Although most people immediately think of green when they hear the word 'jade,' it is also found in colors such as orange, blue, brown, blue-green, cream, lavender, white, and red. It can be translucent (jadeite) or creamy (nephrite).

When you touch jade, there is a peculiar soapy feel.

Rarity

Considered rare, jade is mainly found in Russia, China, Myanmar, the Middle East, and the US. It is formed when myriads of microcrystals interlock with each other in a specific pattern.

The ancient Chinese considered jade only fit for the emperor and it was mined so extensively in China that their deposits of nephrite are almost depleted. However, jadeite is still available.

Uses

Jade, and especially green jade, is seen as a symbol of purity, wisdom, and a calm, clear mind. The Chinese believed it could protect the wearer from spiritual harm, even in the afterlife.

It also helps the wearer to recognize that we are spiritual beings on a human journey, and it opens memories of old wisdom.

Jade promotes self-sufficiency by integrating the mind and body, making problems easier to tackle because new ideas are stimulated in the process.

In the physical sense, jade is used to clean our purifying bodily systems, especially the kidneys and spleen.

Position

Place the stone where it is needed. According to ancient belief, just holding a piece of jade in your hand can transfer its healing properties to anywhere in your body.

Associated Zodiac Sign and Element

Jade is associated with Capricorn, which is an Earth element sign.

* * *

Citrine

Yellow citrine stones among a few scattered green peridots.

The lovely yellow color of citrines brings a feel of sunshine and new life with it. In Greek mythology, citrine was used to honor Persephone, the goddess of spring.

Appearance

Natural citrine is found in yellow, yellowish brown, or smoky gray-brown colors. The crystals are transparent, and they often occur in geodes or clusters, besides single points.

It is one of the few crystals that is self-cleaning; they dissipate negative energy by themselves, so they will remain bright and clear.

Rarity

Citrine is not found in many countries. Furthermore, natural citrine is quite rare. Amethysts are often heat-treated and sold as citrines, so choose a reputable dealer whom you can trust to sell you a genuine citrine crystal.

Uses

Citrine is an energizing stone that cleanses and regenerates us on every level and in a powerful way. It encourages happiness, self-confidence, and calm analysis of situations. Wearing or holding a citrine has helped me to be less sensitive to criticism and to see the constructive side of it.

It is often used to aid the manifestation of wealth and

success, while promoting the sharing of prosperity with those less fortunate.

Citrine works against depression and many self-destructive tendencies, replacing them with motivation and creativity.

Because of its energizing qualities, citrines are used by healers to treat conditions such as chronic fatigue syndrome.

Position

The best results are obtained when your citrine can touch your skin, but it is also effective in a ring or pendant. If you wear a single point, point it downward to pull the positive energy of the cosmos down into the physical plane.

A sphere can be an effective meditation aid, or you can place it in the feng shui wealth corner of your home or business.

Avoid direct sunlight because citrine fades easily.

Associated Zodiac Sign and Element

Citrine is associated with Cancer, Gemini, and Aries. Cancer is a Water element sign, Gemini is associated with the Air element, and Aries is a Fire element sign.

* * *

Hematite

Hematite is believed to be one of the strong stones for protection of the mind, body, and soul. It is often used by psychics and shamans to guide the soul back to the body after an out-of-body experience.

Appearance

Hematite is an iron oxide crystal, resulting in color variations of black, gray, and silver, as well as more reddish-brown hues. It has a natural metallic-like luster.

It is a heavy stone that feels cool to the touch.

Rarity

Hematite is not rare at all, although it is mainly found in European countries.

Uses

In healing, hematite is excellent for boosting self-confidence, willpower, and focus. It can be a great aid to overcome addictions by opening the mind to recognize unfulfilled desires that could be the source of the addiction.

Many people who were treated with hematite crystals have reported being able to see obstacles in their lives as opportunities, rather than disasters, for the first time.

In the physical sense, hematite is strongly connected to our blood. Its name is derived from the Greek word for blood. Hematite is used to regulate blood supply and restore good circulation.

Nightly leg cramps, insomnia, and anxiety are soothed with hematite.

Because of its ability to draw unnecessary heat away from the body, it is also used to break fevers.

It can also help to straighten misaligned spinal discs and speed up the recovery of fractures.

Position

When used for spinal alignment, crystals should be placed at the top and bottom of the spinal column.

For any other purpose, the stones can be placed where they are needed to heal and calm.

A hematite anklet, necklace, or bracelet can keep you within the stone's protective powers all day long.

A pointed hematite crystal in your living space can keep lower vibrations from reaching you.

Associated Zodiac Sign and Element

Hematite is associated with Aries, Scorpio, and Capricorn. Aries is a Fire element sign, Scorpio is the Water element, and Capricorn is an Earth element sign.

Carnelian

A set of jewelry made with polished red carnelian beads.

Another grounding stone, carnelian stabilizes hectic energy and channels it into creativity. If you have any artistic bones in your body, carnelian is your stone.

In ancient times, carnelian crystals were placed on the bodies of the dead to guide them through the afterlife with courage.

Appearance

Carnelian is best known as a red stone, but it can also be pink, orange, or brown. The pebbles are translucent.

Rarity

This is not a rare stone at all; it can be found in countries all over the world.

. . .

Uses

Carnelians burst with vitality and a positive life force, so it is excellent for boosting a sluggish metabolism. Lethargy doesn't stand a chance when carnelian is around!

It is believed to help in overcoming fertility problems, frigidity, and impotence.

Psychologically, it is used to help people overcome their fear of death and accept the natural cycle of life.

On the mental plane, it brings clarity of thought and boosts analytic abilities and concentration.

It can help to overcome anger and frustration, replacing it with a natural, positive zest for life.

Position

Carnelians work well in pendants and belt buckles or worn against the skin when necessary.

Place carnelian near your front door to invite prosperity and provide protection from negativity.

Associated Zodiac Sign and Element

Carnelian is primarily associated with Aries, which is a Fire element sign. However, Virgo and Leo can also benefit from carnelian energies.

Selenite

A beautiful selenite lamp next to a selenite candle holder.

Selenite is a delicate crystal that emits subtle, fine vibrations. It carries within itself an imprint of history and is used to facilitate access to past lives.

It is important to note that selenite cannot be submerged in water. It will dissolve.

Appearance

The best-known version of selenite is pure white, although it can also be found in blue, green, orange, and brown.

The crystals are translucent with ribbing in different formations visible. The white ones, which are known as Satin Spar, have fine ribbing. The ribbing can also be like petals, as in the Desert Rose variety, or in a fishtail pattern.

Rarity

Selenite is easily obtainable in most countries.

Uses

Selenite crystals can open our minds to the higher, angelic consciousness. It is believed to be a link between the higher realms and our physical bodies.

It can be used to create a protective grid around a person or house, warding off negative energy and helping to keep peace reigning inside.

Selenite wands can remove unwanted elements from the aura.

A selenite crystal can clear a confused mind and enhance insight into troubling situations. It sharpens judgment and helps us to understand the subconscious occurrences in our lives.

On a physical level, it is great for maintaining flexibility and can help to straighten a crooked spinal column.

Position

The crystals can be held in the hand or placed against the skin if it won't get wet in any way.

To form a grid, crystals can be placed in the inside corners of a house or around a person's chair or bed.

Associated Zodiac Sign and Element

Selenite is associated with Taurus and Cancer. Taurus is an Earth element sign, while Cancer is a Water element sign.

The Key Takeaways

- There is a huge variety of crystals available, and it can be confusing for beginners.
- This chapter provided a list of 10 crystals that any novice can purchase and use with confidence to start a crystal healing journey.

Chapter 4

Your Guide to Other Essential Crystals

"You can't buy happiness, but you can buy crystals, which is kind of the same thing."

Lewis, n.d.

There are so many wonderful crystals that it is difficult to emphasize some of them while leaving others out.

While experimenting and following your intuition remain the best ways to choose your crystals, there are some that seem to have more universal applications than others.

In this chapter, we'll spend some time with 60 of those stones and crystals, discussing them from various angles. Those that we have already looked at in the previous chapter about the top 10 will only be mentioned if there are additional properties to highlight.

* * *

Agate (The Stone of Plentitude)

Agate is a mineral in the quartz family. It is named after a river in Sicily where the stone was found for the first time, which was around the third or fourth century BCE.

The microscopically small particles of quartz, formed by the absorption of minerals, are arranged in bands that form intricate patterns to which ancient users attached meanings. Many of these exquisitely patterned stones can still be seen in museums and art galleries.

Appearance

Agates appear in all colors, even including a colorless variety. Most of them are clear or milky, but moss agate and dendritic agate are beautiful translucent forms of the stone. The delicately elegant blue lace agate is one of the best-known varieties.

They are soft stones that have a waxy feel.

Agates are commonly found in many countries around the world.

Healing Applications

Agate is used as a powerful cleansing stone at both the emotional and physical levels. It removes negative energy and balances the yin and yang.

When it is placed on the heart, for instance, it can help to heal any emotional scars and residue that prevent us from accepting and giving love. When used on the abdomen, it can clear up a bout of gastritis.

Meditating with an agate can help us get a clear mental picture of who we are. Its peaceful vibrations gently nudge us to accept ourselves. Stones with regular shapes restore harmony, while irregularly shaped stones guide us into action.

All agates, but especially blue lace agates, can calm agitated emotions and anger and restore our composure. That will dissolve tension so we can feel safe and secure again. Through the emotional connection established with the wearer or holder, agates enable us to always stay authentic and humble.

Agates provide a boost for immunity and strengthen our bodies' regenerative powers.

Because of its stabilizing effect on hormones, it is believed that regular use of agates during and after pregnancy can ward off the dreaded "baby blues."

It can alleviate headaches and migraines, as well as any joint or muscle pains.

Red agates are especially suited to clear up digestive issues and boost circulation, the green ones specialize in anti-inflammatory work, and the blue and purple varieties are great for swollen glands and sore throats.

In chakra work, it can stabilize, cleanse, and brighten the whole aura. The color variety of agates means that it can be used on any chakra—just choose the color you want.

Regular travelers, both on land and sea, will benefit from the protection of an agate in the vehicle.

Fire agate is a great aid in meditation, focusing the mind for a deep journey into the self.

Agate is the birthstone for the Zodiac sign of Gemini. It is also the accepted stone for the 12th and 14th wedding anniversaries.

In feng shui, agate can be used to ward off negative energy and dark spirits while drawing in positive energy and helpful spirits.

Care

Agates are durable and do not demand any special treatment. They can be cleansed and recharged in any way that is convenient for you.

They vibrate at a relatively low frequency, so you can have them around you every day.

* * *

Amazonite (The Stone of Courage and Truth)

This is another classic ancient Egyptian beauty, along with lapis lazuli, turquoise, and carnelian. The soft turquoise green that is the main color in amazonite represented rebirth in the afterlife to the Egyptians.

They called the stone *neshmet*, but the word was difficult for Westerners to remember. Instead, it was renamed in more recent times to evoke pictures of the lush green rainforest at the equator.

. . .

Appearance

Amazonite is a form of the mineral feldspar. It is found all over the world with excellent deposits in the Pikes Peak area of Colorado, US.

The stones are mostly opalescent, shot through with veins of white, gray, or yellow.

Healing Applications

Amazonites are mainly filters and soothers.

They are the go-to stones for protection against electromagnetic vibrations and geopathic stress; some people tape an amazonite to their mobile phones.

The stone soothes anxiety and stress and clears the mind to see other sides of a problem too. It encourages open and loving communication because it works on the throat and heart chakras.

On the physical plane, amazonite is used to ease the pain and discomfort of osteoporosis. It can also help to relieve muscle spasms and rectify calcium deficiencies.

Amazonite contains low levels of lead and should not be ingested as an elixir.

Care

This is a soft stone that can scratch and break easily. Never put it in an ultrasonic cleaner and do not expose the stone to harsh chemicals.

It does not do well in high temperatures either, so store your amazonite in a cool place.

Keep them separate from other stones to prevent scratching and chipping.

* * *

Amber (The Stone of the Sun)

This lovely, fossilized resin, with its rich golden color, has been used as a crystal for so long now that it's easy to forget it is not really a gemstone or a mineral. Amber comes from a species of coniferous trees that grew more than thirty million years ago, but that is now extinct.

It is highly regarded as a grounding stone due to its intimate connection to the earth.

Appearance

Amber's natural colors are brown, deep orange, and yellow. Other shades, such as blue or green, are usually artificially obtained, although there have been specimens that naturally occurred in green, red, or blue.

It can be opaque or transparent, with insects or pieces of vegetation sometimes trapped inside. Stones with inclusions are deemed powerful and are highly desirable.

Amber is easily obtainable but most of it comes from the coasts of the Baltic and North Seas.

. . .

Healing Applications

As long ago as the Stone Age, amber was used to treat illness and bring peace to the mind. Some of the descriptions used through the ages were drops of sunlight solidified, hardened honey, and tears of the gods.

It is credited with the ability to draw stagnant, negative energy out from the body and mind, transforming it into clear, positive vibrations. It also kickstarts the body's own healing potential.

Amber is often used specifically to protect and heal children and the elderly.

Pieces placed around a living space can purify the atmosphere and serve as a shield to keep the energy positive after clearing.

The yellow tones in amber make it a good stone to work on the solar plexus chakra.

Care

Because amber is only resin, it is soft and porous. It should never be placed in an ultrasonic cleaner or cleaned with any chemicals. Simply wipe your stones with a damp cloth and let them dry away from direct sunlight.

Angelite (The Stone of Awareness)

Also known as angel stone or anhydrite, angelite is a common mineral first discovered in Lima, Peru. It is formed when large bodies of seawater evaporate.

In their natural state, the bluish-gray stones are often shaped like wings.

Appearance

Angelite is opaque and found in blue or gray varieties, streaked through with white. Some stones are flecked with red.

Besides Peru, the mineral can be found in Poland, Egypt, Germany, Britain, Mexico, and Libya.

Healing Applications

As can be deduced from the name, crystal workers often use the stone as a connector to the angelic realm and to enhance telepathic communication.

It awakens genuine compassion to bring about wholeness again and unblock all energetic channels.

When applied to the feet, angelite can resonate with the throat to alleviate thyroid issues and calm inflammation.

Its balancing and purifying properties also makes angelite a great diuretic.

Care

Angelite is a soft, delicate stone that should never be cleaned with chemicals or put in an ultrasonic cleaner.

Store it away from other, harder stones to prevent damage.

* * *

Apatite (The Stone of Inspiration and Motivation)

Apatite is the name of a series of three minerals—fluorapatite, chlorapatite, and hydroxylapatite—that form the apatite group. The stones are usually a combination of all three.

Appearance

Apatite crystals can be glassy or opaque. Their colors range from blue, green, and yellow to brown, pink, and violet. The blue variety is readily available with weights exceeding five carats. The yellow stones are rarer.

The overall color effect is always on the cooler side of the color wheel, even with warmer colors such as brown and yellow.

The color of a gemstone largely determines its price. The rarest color is neon, sometimes described as electric blue or swimming pool blue. A good-sized chunk, if it is larger than one carat, can set you back up to $180 per carat.

Healing Applications

It is a good aid to sharpen concentration and focus and enhance creativity.

Its healing properties can benefit bone growth, teeth health, and new cell formation greatly. It can relieve pain from arthritis and any other joint problems.

Apatite can speed up the metabolism while suppressing hunger, making it a good stone for weight loss.

It reduces irritability and anger and fills our emotional energy reserves again with positive, productive passion for life.

Care

Apatite is moderately soft and can withstand more bumps than some of the other stones. They are, however, porous and should never be put into an ultrasonic cleaner or cleaned with abrasive chemicals.

* * *

Aquamarine (The Stone of Communication)

Aquamarines look like their name suggests. The word is made up from the Latin words "aqua marinus," which mean "water of the sea." Looking at a clear, sparkling aquamarine will have you thinking about relaxing Mediterranean waters in no time.

Ancient sailors took aquamarines on their voyages as protection because they thought the stones were gifts from mermaids.

. . .

Appearance

Aquamarines range in color from light blue to turquoise and teal—indeed, all the hues of seawater are represented. Staring into one of them can instantly remind us of sunshine sparkling on the eternal blue water of the sea.

They can be clear or opaque.

Healing Applications

Because of the strong association with the sea, aquamarines are believed to have an immense amount of energy to impart, especially for all types of communicators such as teachers and coaches. Some public speakers won't go on stage without an aquamarine in their pocket.

The aquamarine energy will bring your words in sync with the flow of the mood you want to communicate, working through the power of the throat chakra. Stage fright will be something of the past and you'll be able to stay true to the words you want to say.

The stone can shelter our emotions, so that it is easier to remain optimistic about life. At the same time, it can clear our mental processes and prevent overthinking.

With regards to physical healing, swollen glands, sore throats and thyroid problems can be relieved with the help of an aquamarine. It strengthens and tones the body's cleansing organs and calms upset immune systems.

Care

No special care is needed. The stones are quite hard and not porous.

Azurite (The Stone of Heaven)

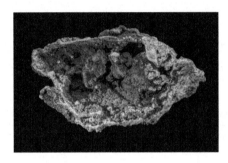

Beautiful azurite combined with other minerals to create a beautiful composition in nature.

This deep blue mineral is named for its brilliant color. Centuries ago, painters used azurite to make their blue paint because they could not find anything more perfect.

Azurite likes to team up with malachite in nature; the resulting mineral is known as azurite malachite, or azurmalachite for short.

Appearance

Azurite crystals are small and, when tumbled, the stones are also quite small. They become shiny in the tumbling process, accentuating the deep blue color.

They are not rare at all and countries including the US, South America, Namibia, and Egypt have deposits.

Healing Applications

Azurite resonates perfectly with the indigo blue of the third eye chakra. It expands the mind to nudge it toward full spiritual enlightenment. It stimulates the intellect while bringing it into line with psychic perspectives.

It is an excellent stone for deep meditation, out-of-body experiences, and channeling. The effects will be enhanced when used in conjunction with music such as Buddhist or Gregorian chants, choral music, drums, and the didgeridoo.

The stone can soften grief and sadness, helping us to understand why we had to go through these experiences.

Physically, azurite works on spinal alignment and joint issues. It also helps with detoxification and blood circulation.

When in combination with malachite, both the detoxifying effect and the awakening effect on the third eye are amplified.

Care

Both azurite and malachite are highly toxic due to high levels of copper. Both minerals are soluble in acid and ammonia too, so take great care when handling them.

Wear a face mask and don't inhale the dust while cutting the stones. They are soft and dust will be plentiful. Don't immerse them in water and never drink any liquid that held azurite and/or malachite. Keep them away from any abrasive materials and ultrasonic cleaners.

Cavansite (The Stone of Spiritual Direction)

A magnificent piece of cavansite.

The name of this striking blue mineral is derived from its chemical components: calcium, vanadium, and silicon. It's only been known since the 1960s. It is rare and highly sought after, occurring only in Oregon, US (where it was first found), Brazil, Iceland, New Zealand, and India.

Appearance

Cavansite forms rosette-like clusters in all the shades of brilliant blue you can think of, including a fabulous aqua green color.

The crystals are transparent with an innate soft luster.

. . .

Healing Applications

Cavansite works to cure sore throats, alleviate eye problems, and ease tinnitus. It works on the cellular level to help our bodies heal right from our core.

On a psychic level, it enhances intuition and shields a healer from negative energy during a healing session.

If you are perhaps about to relocate and you're not sure if the ambiance in the new house will be friendly and relaxed, cavansite can clear the air and invite positivity in.

It is an excellent aid during meditation or to interpret dreams. The stone works on all three the upper chakras, aligning us to the heavenly realms.

Those of us born under the zodiac sign of Aquarius will find cavansite especially energizing.

Care

If you can get hold of some cavansite, it will be worth your while to treat it carefully. It is a soft stone that can scratch easily.

Submersion in any kind of liquid is not recommended. Cavansite's structure is brittle and water seeping into any small cracks can widen the cracks enough for the stone to break apart.

Wear a mask when cutting or grinding cavansite because silicon and vanadium can be harmful when the dust is breathed in.

* * *

Celestite (The Stone of Heavenly Communication)

The name celestite is derived from the Latin word for heaven, *coelestis*. The mainly sky-blue color of the stone reminded people since early times of the heavens, elevating their thoughts to the universe.

The mineral is also known as celestine.

Appearance

Celestite forms pyramidical transparent crystals in yellow, blue, white, light red, green, brown, and colorless varieties.

It is easy to get hold of celestite, but it can be quite costly.

Healing Applications

The high frequency at which celestite vibrates makes it an excellent teacher stone. It forms a bridge between our consciousness and the infinite peace of the higher realms. Any spiritual development can be fast tracked through regular medi-tation with celestite.

Dysfunctional relationships will also benefit from this stone because it restores harmony and opens channels for peaceful negotiations. It reconnects our intellect with our instinctive knowledge to bring balance and tranquility.

Anyone suffering from panic attacks will also benefit from celestite's ability to center and ground us, restoring the feeling of being safe.

On the physical level, celestite can treat the ears and eyes, help with detoxification, and ease muscle tension. It will also alleviate digestive issues brought on by tension.

Care

Celestite is not hard and will get scratched easily. The softness makes it soluble in hot acids or alkali carbonate solutions, and it should be kept away from water too.

Keep the colored varieties out of direct sunlight and away from heat sources to avoid bleaching.

* * *

Chalcedony (The Speaker's Stone)

Resonating with the throat chakra, chalcedony, and especially the blue variety, is a communicator's assistant. It is a variety of quartz that can be roughly divided again into agates and jaspers.

Appearance

Chalcedony can be transparent or opaque. The main colors are gray, blue, white, red, and pink. The appearance can be banded.

The natural stones are evenly colored and rather pale, so if you find a stone that's garish and bright, you're likely dealing with a fake.

It is a common mineral found in numerous countries.

Healing Applications

Sore throats, congested chests, and inflammation in the throat and mouth area can be alleviated with chalcedony. If you suffer from a toothache, chalcedony can also provide some relief.

This crystal can be used to help you voice your true feelings with courage, and in turn, to listen better to others.

Its energy is lighthearted, bringing stress relief with a smile.

Care

Chalcedony is quite hard and does not need too much special care, although any dyed stones should be kept away from harsh chemicals and ultrasonic cleaners.

The stone can be affected by perspiration when worn against the skin, especially for those people with acidic perspiration.

It has a low risk of causing silicosis when the dust is inhaled.

* * *

Charoite (The Stone of Metamorphosis)

Charoite is a silicate mineral that is named after the river Chara in Russia's Sakha Republic, where it was discovered the first time in the late 1940s.

It only reached the Western markets in 1978, largely

because it is not eye-catching in its raw form.

Appearance

Charoite is a mottled, veined stone with swirls of charcoal or khaki contained in the crystal. The main color varies from dark purple to lilac to light pink.

It is rare and the only known source so far is in a specific geological formation in Russia.

Healing Applications

This is a stone that is bursting with the vibrant energy of love and transformation. It integrates energy on all levels to gain divine insight and live authentically. It inspires compassion and kindness.

It is a good painkiller, stress buster, and blood pressure regulator. Charoite renews our energy when we are ill or stressed and makes sure we get a good night's sleep.

Care

This is a medium-hard stone, but it is sensitive to hard pressure and heat. Mild soap, lukewarm water, and a soft brush will be enough to clean your charoite.

It is sensitive to acid, so be careful when there is a chance of perspiration touching the stone.

Danburite

The first danburite was discovered in 1839 in Danbury, Connecticut, USA. Since then, deposits have also been found in Mexico, Russia, Japan, Madagascar, and Burma.

It is easy to confuse danburite and quartz with each other, but danburite has a unique crystal structure that makes it harder than quartz.

Appearance

Danburite is mostly colorless but can also be found as pale-yellow to brownish-yellow stones.

They are transparent to translucent crystals.

Although danburite itself is not rare, finding large pieces is a rare occurrence.

Healing Applications

These crystals have a high vibration that works well with the crown chakra. They lift our spirits and link our intellect with the heart chakra.

Danburite is an excellent meditation aid.

It calms feelings that have been stirred up by disagreements and misunderstandings, restoring patience and calm.

On the physical level, danburite clears allergies and helps to detoxify our bodies by supporting the liver.

. . .

Care

Danburite is exceptionally hard compared to most other stones, but it can still get scratched easily. Store your danburites on their own.

Ultrasonic cleaning is safe, but danburite is quite sensitive to heat. Avoid any steam cleaning, as well as huge shifts in temperature. A good wipe with a soft cloth and room-temperature water is all your stones need to be clean and ready once more.

* * *

Emerald (The Stone of Successful Love)

Emeralds don't need an introduction. Their green brilliance has been known throughout history and has been held in high esteem by many dynasties all over the world. The Chaldeans, who are described in the Christian Bible, even believed their goddess Ishtar lived inside the stones.

The name emerald comes from as far back as the Sanskrit word *marakata*, meaning "spring green."

Appearance

Emeralds are small, shiny green gemstones, while the crystals are more cloudy. They are expensive but not too difficult to obtain.

Sources include India, Brazil, Tanzania, Zimbabwe, Egypt, and Austria.

. . .

Healing Applications

The rich green color symbolizes new life and love. It empowers the heart chakra to manifest pure love in the physical world.

It sharpens our intuition and can awaken any latent prophetic gifts.

In feng shui, emeralds have become associated with money and wealth because of their color.

The stone can aid recovery from infections of any sort and bring relief from the relentless pain of rheumatism.

It is also said to boost physical eyesight just as much as it opens our minds' eye.

The symbolic new growth of the green stone is manifested physically in fertility and successful pregnancies for the wearer.

Care

Emeralds can scratch and shatter quickly and easily. A soft cloth and warmish water will clean them without any risk.

They also do not like huge temperature changes.

Heliodor (The Stone of the Sun)

Named by the Greeks as a "gift from the sun" for its bright yellow color, heliodor is an intriguing form of the mineral beryl.

It was first discovered in 1912 in Namibia and is sometimes called golden beryl.

Appearance

Heliodor ranges in color from pale yellow to dark, orangey yellow. Some stones even have a greenish tint to them.

Their main natural formation is in the form of long, thin rods with etchings.

The stone has only been found in Namibia, Madagascar, and Brazil, making it rare.

Healing Applications

Heliodor is associated with the solar plexus chakra. As such, it can help to establish a bridge between our intellectual minds and our emotions. With the help of heliodor, both men and women can become more assertive and confident, but always tempered with wisdom.

Physically, it can strengthen our immune systems. When we encounter objects that were in the presence of sick people, heliodor energy can purify the items.

This stone is often called upon to cleanse and heal the liver, spleen, and pancreas. It can calm digestive disorders and relieve constipation.

Care

Golden beryl is quite hard, but the inclusions that cause the distinctive etchings might be more vulnerable to knocks.

Only use lukewarm water and a soft brush to clean heliodor, avoiding cleaning agents.

The color can fade when exposed to direct sunlight for too long.

* * *

Herkimer Diamond (The Stone of Attunement)

The clear and sparkling Herkimer diamond is a form of quartz first discovered in Herkimer county, New York. Workmen cutting stone in the Mohawk River Valley found it in the 18th century and geologists estimate its age to be more than 500 million years.

Appearance

These beautiful quartz crystals are mostly clear, but they can range from just transparent to hazy. They usually occur double-ended in nature, but other forms are possible.

Healing Applications

If you need a stone to ease your mind in an uncomfortable situation, reach for a Herkimer diamond. Its high vibrations will stabilize you and point you in the right direction if any action is needed. The double-ended structure makes it possible for the crystal to absorb the destabilizing energy on one end while directing grounding vibrations to you from the other end.

For our bodies, Herkimer diamonds are great detoxifiers. They can also provide a shield against electromagnetic stress.

Care

All quartz is robust, but don't expose the crystals to high temperatures or big changes in temperature.

They can be immersed in water for cleaning purposes but not for making elixirs, as the silicone content of the stones is too high.

Howlite (The Stone of Tolerance)

Howlite was named after Henry How, the mineralogist who discovered it in 1868 in Southern California. It is usually found in the borax deposits of the US's desert regions. Although the mineral has since been found in Turkey, Serbia, and Germany too, California and Nevada in the US are the only sites where it was ever found in its crystallized form.

The stone is also known as magnesite.

Appearance

Howlite is a beautiful white stone with a marbled appearance. The veins are usually dark gray but can also be brown or black.

It has a soft natural luster that reminds me of a delicate piece of old porcelain.

Fake alert: howlite is often dyed to look like turquoise. Check the hardness of the stone you want to purchase, especially if the color looks exceptionally bright. Turquoise is a brittle, soft stone that doesn't work well in jewelry. The gem market started selling dyed howlite as so-called "hardened turquoise."

Healing Applications

This gemstone with its fine dark veins may look mild and soft, but the energy it packs is formidable. Howlite can quickly calm an angry, stormy mind to bring us back to a more tolerant point of view.

It is an excellent stone to silence the daily noise in our heads, so it is possible to adopt a more mindful lifestyle. Overactive imaginations can find rest and the worry knots in our stomachs can safely untangle.

On a physiological plane, howlite helps to regulate the calcium content in our bones.

It is associated with the water element and can alert us when we need more fluids to function well and stay calm and focused.

Care

Howlite is not a hard stone, so take care when storing it with other crystals. Keep it away from perspiration, chemicals, and acids, as its calcium structure does not stand up to these hazards.

It can go into water for short periods, but not be immersed and left there.

Iolite (The Stone of Vision)

This stone's nickname comes from the incredible violet color that is dominant, making it a favorite for working with the higher chakras.

It is the gemstone variety of the mineral cordierite and is also known as water sapphire. Although it is difficult to work with for lapidaries, it is a popular gemstone because it is so much cheaper than real sapphires.

Appearance

Violet is predominant but blue, gray, and yellow iolites, as well as some colorless examples, have been found. They are translucent stones that are usually small in size.

Iolites play with light due to the optical phenomenon known as pleochroism. This means the color changes depending on the angle and the external source of light. Viking sailors used the gemstones as polarizing aids to find their way in overcast conditions.

The stone's popularity is growing but it is still not widely obtainable.

Healing Applications

Because of its association with light and finding your way, it was perhaps unavoidable that iolite should become a go-to stone for opening the third eye. Many shamans prefer iolite to give them clear visions on their journeys.

It brings insight and understanding of our true selves, so that we can release all patterns and habits that sabotage our greatness.

On the physical level, treatment with iolites can help the body to reduce harmful fatty deposits and strengthen overall. It can also assist with detoxification of the liver.

Care

Iolite is a hard and durable stone, and no special care is needed, besides keeping it away from steam and ultrasonic cleaners.

* * *

Jasper (The Nurturing Stone)

Jasper is a collective name for a group of chalcedony quartz crystals. The name means "speckled or spotted gemstone" from the Latin word *iaspis*.

. . .

Appearance

The stone's name sums the appearance of all the jasper varieties up perfectly. They are found in a wide variety of colors that are flecked with other colors and livened up by swirls and lines in other colors that are caused by inclusions of other minerals. The main colors are brown, red, yellow, and orange.

These stones can be found all over the world and they are known by many different names, according to their colors.

Healing Applications

Jasper is associated with the circulatory and digestive systems, supporting our natural regenerative functions.

It is also used for recuperating patients to re-energize their bodies without overstimulating them.

Metaphysically, the jaspers are associated with the root chakra. It provides support, both to our physical bodies and our mental endeavors.

It can restore calm and ground our emotions, helping us to throw away emotional baggage.

Care

This is a tough stone, and no special care is needed, unless the stones you are working with are dyed.

* * *

Jet (The Stone of Protection)

Just like amber, jet is not a gemstone, but it has been used for so long in crystal healing that it is firmly entrenched as such.

Jet is petrified wood, almost like coal. It has been around a long time; the oldest artifacts made from jet that archeologists found date from the Bronze Age.

The Romans wore jet talismans to ward off the evil eye and chase snakes away.

Appearance

Both hard jet that was formed in salt water and soft jet that formed in fresh water are pitch black. It can be polished to a great shine.

In its raw form, jet looks like coal or bark. It is easily obtainable.

Healing Applications

Jet is credited with high protective powers, due to its connection to the earth. It purifies and draws in positive energy.

Migraines and colds can be treated with jet because it reduces glandular swelling.

Jet also makes an excellent cleaner and charger for other crystals. Cover the crystals with pieces of jet and leave them for a couple of hours. However, take care when covering the crystals to avoid any of them scratching each other.

. . .

Care

When working with jet, always remember that you're holding a piece of organic material. It is soft on the Moh Scale and cannot be cleaned with anything abrasive.

Never use steam or ultrasonic cleaners on jet; lukewarm water and a soft cloth will do.

Kunzite (The Stone of Emotion)

Kunzite is a pinkish purple stone that is sometimes called "the woman's stone" because of its feminine-type beauty.

Nobody is quite sure exactly who discovered it, but it was named in 1903 after the gemologist and mineralogist George Frederick Kunz, who verified it as a new variety of the mineral spodumene.

Appearance

Kunzite's color range stretches from pale, pastel pink to intense, bright violet. It has a lovely sparkle when polished.

The main deposits are in Pakistan and Afghanistan, but Brazil, the US, and Madagascar also have some quantities. It is becoming easier to get hold of kunzite.

Healing Applications

Kunzite is strongly associated with joyful love, straight from the heart without strings attached. The stone is said to make it easy to reciprocate love without fearing heartache.

It also opens the heart to be gentle and compassionate toward all creatures, nature, and ourselves.

Although kunzite looks like it belongs to the crown chakra, it is, in fact, better suited to the heart chakra. Spodumene in its base form is green, which is the color of the fourth chakra.

In the physical sense, kunzite strengthens the heart muscle and optimizes blood circulation. It can also boost the immune system and ease joint pain.

Care

The colors of this stone are vulnerable to sunlight and UV rays; there have been numerous reports of kunzite fading completely when it was left out in the sun.

Handle it gently when cleaning as well as during healing sessions because it is a moderately soft stone.

✳ ✳ ✳

Kyanite (The Stone of Clarity)

Since the discovery of this mineral in 1879, it was only used industrially until the bright blue variety that is so popular today was found in Nepal in the late 1990s.

Since then, several other colors were also found.

The name is derived from the Greek word for blue, *kyanos*.

Appearance

The crystal is layered with a sheen ranging from glassy to more like pearls. Pink, yellow, green, orange, gray, and black varieties have been found. Sometimes the colors are streaked with white.

The main source is Brazil, but it is not difficult to obtain kyanite anywhere. The finest blue and blue-green specimens can, however, get pricey.

Healing Applications

Kyanite is often used in meditation and during attunements. It acts as a transmitter and amplifier of energy.

It aligns all the chakras at the same time with a nurturing and soothing vibration, leaving you with a bubbling feeling of happiness.

It boosts our physical regenerative powers to alleviate pain, dissipate tension, and clear up infections.

Care

This is a medium-hard stone that is prone to split along the visible grain, so treat it with care. Don't use abrasive or harsh materials on it and never put it in an ultrasonic or steam cleaner.

* * *

Labradorite (The Stone of Mysticism)

There are few stones with a more mystical quality than the family of iridescent labradorites. Think for a moment about the magical glow of color that seems to float inside a moonstone, and you'll understand.

Labradorite is a type of feldspar and was first found in the Canadian province of Labrador. According to legend, Inuits thought the Northern Lights were trapped in the rocks.

Appearance

Labradorite is made up of various layers of minerals and the different layers create the play of light. All the colors of the rainbow can be seen in labradorite stones.

It is a common stone in most countries.

Healing Applications

Healers use labradorite for ailments of the eyes and to regulate blood pressure. It is also beneficial for wound healing.

It is also great for relieving congestion due to colds and flu.

In the metaphysical sense, labradorite in all its forms can sharpen our sixth sense, boost our sense of self, enhance wisdom, and help to create success. It calms a racing mind so that we can connect our left and right brain hemispheres to arrive at the best solution to any problem.

It also affords protection when we journey into higher spiritual realms.

. . .

Care
Labradorite is medium hard but should not be steam cleaned or scrubbed with bleach or other abrasive elements.

* * *

Lapis Lazuli (The Stone of Wisdom)

Nothing spells royalty like lapis lazuli. This stone is more than 6,500 years old and has always been held in high esteem, and not only for its luscious blue color. We have numerous historic records of lapis being used in ancient rituals.

Renaissance painters used the finely ground stone to create a pigment called ultramarine.

Appearance
Lapis is a dense, deep blue stone with a veined appearance. It has been described as looking like a map of the night sky with its golden inclusions due to the pyrite content.

This is not a rare gemstone, but good quality specimens are quite expensive. The price decreases when the stone contains a lot of white.

Healing Applications
Famous for its power to awaken and open the third eye,

lapis lazuli is generally regarded as one of the best stones for enlightenment and spiritual journeys.

It inspires truthful self-expression, facilitates effective communication, and enhances intuition.

Lapis can bring relief from physical pain, especially in the case of migraines.

Being associated with the throat chakra, it can benefit the whole respiratory system and the thyroid.

Care

Lapis is a porous stone, and it is made up of several different minerals. That makes it vulnerable to damage from various sides.

It is soft so it can chip and scratch easily, while chemicals and the vibrations of ultrasonic cleaners will break its structure apart.

* * *

Larimar (The Stone of the Sea)

Larimar is a new kid on the gemstone block. It was first discovered in 1974 in the Dominican Republic. A local resident, Miguel Mendez, actively promoted the stone and named it after his daughter, Larissa, and the Spanish word for the sea, 'mar.'

Other names for this dreamy blue stone are dolphin stone, Caribbean gemstone, and Atlantis stone.

Appearance

The stone is a rare blue variety of the grayish-white mineral pectolite. The color comes from the inclusions of calcium instead of cobalt, as in regular pectolite. The swirling bands of white through the blue stone look just like the wave crests in the blue Caribbean sea.

The only major larimar mine in the world is in the remote mountains of Barahona in the Dominican Republic. Residents pry the stones from the narrow crevices using only primitive hand tools. Despite the hard work involved, it is surprisingly easy to get hold of larimar in gemstone shops.

Healing Applications

Larimar stimulates all the top chakras and works specifically on the throat to improve communication.

It can soothe stress and is often used for worry stones, especially during meditation.

Some people believe that larimar can reduce a fear of flying.

Healers also use larimar to calm high fevers and reduce inflammation.

Care

Larimar is a soft stone that requires gentle handling and cleaning. The color can fade completely if it gets exposed to intense heat or chemicals.

It can tolerate water but avoid submerging it for prolonged periods.

* * *

Lepidolite (The Stone of Peace)

If you are looking for a stone to help you detach from the daily noise to focus on what is important, lepidolite is one of your best bets. It will balance all the racing sensations in your mind and unite them to soothe the feeling of being all jumbled up.

Appearance

Lepidolite is part of the mica mineral family, and its rich lithium content gives it a scaly, plate-like appearance. The color is a rich, peaceful maroon-purple to pink.

It can be found in Brazil, Madagascar, the US, the Czech Republic, and the Dominican Republic.

Lepidolite is sometimes also called lithium mica or lilalite.

Healing Applications

The gentle, nurturing vibrations emanating from lepidolite can locate the source of a disease and gently stimulate the body to start healing itself. It strengthens the immune system at the same time and relieves allergies.

If you're suddenly faced with an outbreak of acne, lepidolite can also help to detoxify the skin.

Lepidolite can guide us to deep tranquility, allowing our minds to focus on eternal truths to find answers to modern questions. It is an ultra-calming stone.

Care

You'll have to be gentle with your lepidolite stones, as they are soft and brittle. Never store them with other stones to avoid scratching and only clean them with a soft, moist cloth.

* * *

Magnesite (The Stone of Deep Peace)

Due to its high magnesium content, magnesite has long been a favorite material for making carved ornaments. Native Americans in California also used the beads as a currency and for jewelry.

It is often dyed and substituted for other stones, such as turquoise.

Appearance

Magnesite contains calcium and manganese, among other minerals, giving it a chalky white color with an unglazed porcelain-like appearance. Other colors are yellow, brown, and gray.

The marbled form is readily available but finding magnesite in a crystalline form is rare.

The main sources of this stone are the US and Brazil.

Healing Applications

Magnesite is naturally drawn to the magnesium in our bodies, and it helps us to absorb the mineral fully. In doing so, it strengthens our teeth and bones and may help to prevent epileptic fits.

It also helps to neutralize body odors.

Stressed, tight muscles will find relief using magnesite and headaches will also clear.

When used during meditation, magnesite facilitates visualization and stimulates the imagination.

It works on the heart chakra, so self-esteem also benefits from the use of magnesite.

Care

Magnesite is soft and will break easily. Wipe your stones with a soft, dry cloth and store them apart from each other in a soft pouch.

Keep acid away from magnesite, as it is soluble.

Malachite (The Stone of Transformation)

The mesmerizing green swirls of malachite.

This striking mineral is one of the first ever used to produce copper, but even before that, the Egyptians utilized malachite as a popular cosmetic. The stones were ground to a fine dust and mixed with kohl to produce a striking green eye shadow that was said to be Cleopatra's favorite.

Renaissance painters also mixed ground malachite with their paints to make a vivid green hue.

Appearance

Once you've seen a brilliant green malachite, you'll never forget it again. Bands of light green and bluish green swirl through the dark green stone, sometimes forming rosettes. The green is the result of the copper in the stone that tarnishes.

Malachite is readily obtainable.

. . .

Healing Applications

Malachite is renowned in the crystal world for its ability to absorb pain into itself. The stone is sometimes called the essence of joy because it enables us to transcend pain and find perspective again.

It helps us move through transitions in our lives and empowers us for a great new start.

On the physical level, malachite is quite versatile. It can ease cramps, lower blood pressure, promote bone growth after breaks, and relieve the pain caused by arthritis.

Care

Due to its high copper content, working with malachite can be dangerous. Wear a face mask when cutting or grounding the stone and do not prepare elixirs with it.

The stone is soft despite its widespread use in jewelry, so treat it gently.

Moldavite (The Stone of Connectedness)

If you find a piece of moldavite, you truly have a piece of the stars in your hand. Moldavite is a type of molten glass that is formed during meteorite impacts with the earth.

It was first found in the 1700s near the Moldau River in what is now known as the Czech Republic. Since then, moldavite has only been found in Austria.

. . .

Appearance

Moldavite occurs in all shades of green, from pale to deep, forest green. It is usually opaque but the rare instance of transparent moldavite is extremely valuable.

It is a costly stone to mine because it was formed in the Miocene era, meaning that it is now buried deep in the earth.

The price has been pushed up further by the limited quantities of moldavite available on earth. This has opened opportunities for fraudsters to produce fake moldavite, so beware before you buy. Always deal with reputable retailers.

Healing Applications

Moldavite can be a terrifically intense stone for people who align with its energy. They sense the connection between our world and the universe immediately and some report feeling a burning sensation in the hand holding the stone.

Using moldavite for treatments without some previous experience in crystal healing has been likened to entering the Olympic Games before running a single 100-meter race—it can be an overwhelming experience. If you find it too difficult in the beginning, keep a grounding stone close-by until you're more used to moldavite's energy.

It is a powerful stone that brings about transformation and accelerates personal change. The energy draws out our deepest feelings, helping us to recover from buried trauma and release whatever does not serve us anymore.

. . .

Care

Although moldavite once fell thousands of miles to the earth, it is still glass and can get damaged easily by other stones and abrasive materials.

Wipe your moldavites with a soft, damp cloth and dry them off with another soft cloth before storing your stones in their own velvet pouch.

Morganite (The Stone of Innocence)

Meet the peachy-pink sisters of emeralds, named after the famous banker J. P. Morgan in the early 1900s.

Morganite is also known as pink beryl.

Appearance

Morganite is essentially colorless, but the presence of magnesium creates the pinkish hue. The colors can range from soft pink to peach, right through to salmon when iron is present.

It is excellent in jewelry and has become popular in recent years. Fakes have, unfortunately, also proliferated in the gem market. Always choose a reputable dealer.

Although morganite is found in many countries around the world, it is always in limited quantities at specific locations. It only grows in the company of other minerals.

. . .

Healing Applications

This beautiful stone resonates perfectly with the heart chakra, reminding us to open to innocent, pure love. It lightens our step with the joy of loving who we are and living up to our potential.

Morganite can quickly dissipate stress and bring our frazzled nervous systems back into balance. It boosts energy and mental clarity.

Care

Morganite is medium-hard but cannot tolerate too much heat. Clean your morganites with a mild soap and room temperature water.

Wipe the stones with a soft, dry cloth after washing and allow them to become completely dry before storing them.

* * *

Muscovite (The Stone of Insight)

Muscovite has a long history, going back to the mid-1500s. It was then known as Muscovy glass because Russians in the Muscovy province used the clear sheets as windows.

Appearance

The stone is a type of mica that is highly sought after by collectors. The colors range from yellow, brown, and gray to red, green, and white. Colorless specimens have also been found.

Other names for muscovite are fuchsite and isinglass.

Healing Applications

Even though it is not used as windows any longer, muscovite still gives us insight into the psychic world. It attunes us to the highest energies through its own high vibrations and expands our powers to connect to the divine realm.

It is a great stone for opening the third eye that can be used by all levels of crystal healers. Its energies are not overwhelming but still powerful.

Care

Muscovite is an extremely soft stone and great care should be taken with it.

Obsidian

Obsidian has a long and illustrious history, going as far back as the Stone Age, of being used to make tools and weapons. Highly polished pieces of obsidian also served as early mirrors.

Because of its extremely sharp cutting edge, obsidian is still used to make special blades used in cardiac surgery—the edge of an obsidian blade is only about 3 nanometers wide and completely smooth.

The stone is credited with much power due to its rapid process of formation; it is viscous lava that cooled so quickly after the volcanic eruption that the minerals had no time to form crystals.

Appearance

Obsidian is usually black, brown, or gray with a glassy luster to the opaque stone. Dark green, red, and blue obsidian is extremely rare. Almost colorless varieties have also been found.

The color depends on the inclusions because some stones have tiny gas bubbles trapped in them. The best-known variety with bubbles is called snowflake obsidian; the white mineral cristobalite causes patterns that resemble snowflakes.

Obsidian occurs in all countries that have seen volcanic activity. The dark varieties are readily obtainable in shops.

Healing Applications

Healers use obsidian to show them the cause of a disease.

It also detoxifies and promotes effective digestion, both physically and mentally, to process difficult experiences.

Obsidian will clear negativity out of our auras and provide psychic protection. It can be used to access past-life memories to remove residual trauma.

The stone can also reawaken our creativity and refocus our minds.

. . .

Care

Obsidian is medium hard, and care should be taken to avoid falls or hard knocks.

It can be immersed in water or washed under running water, but do not leave it in the water for prolonged periods. The color has been known to fade from too much water.

Onyx

Onyx has been used in several ancient civilizations to make pottery and jewelry. It is also mentioned frequently in the Bible and was one of the types of precious stones King David used in his new temple.

Appearance

Onyx is a type of chalcedony that naturally occurs as black or dark brown stones with lighter bands. The stones are frequently dyed to either enhance or eliminate the banding, so beware of fakes.

They polish up to a lovely shine.

Healing Applications

The stone is recommended for healthy teeth, bones, and bone marrow. Its strengthening properties also make it useful to combat blood disorders and replenish physical stamina.

Onyx is believed to hold on to the memories of the previous wearer. This makes it a valuable tool when working with someone to heal past traumas and grief.

Care

Clean your onyx stones with a soft, damp cloth and don't put them in ultrasonic or steam cleaners.

Opal

Opals are known as the queens of gemstones because of their incredible variety of color combinations. It is a wide family of stones, but they share the most important traits.

Appearance

Some opals are white with patterns of color, while others provide a dark backdrop to the colorful patterns. The white stones are known as milky opals and the dark ones are black opals.

White opals are the most common, but they can be expensive. Black opals are the rarest and can only be found in Australia.

The rainbow of colors come from tiny spheres of silica that get included into the stone. Each sphere reflects light differently.

Fire opals consist of only one color, but the quality of the color is vivid and fiery.

Healing Applications

If you find yourself forgetting where you put your car keys a bit too often, try strengthening your memory by carrying or wearing an opal. Many people believe that opals not only boost short term memory, but also help to fight the long-term consequences of diseases, such as Parkinson's.

It is also regarded as beneficial for eye disorders and kidney problems.

Psychologically, an opal frees our imaginations and spontaneous creativity. It enhances passion, both for love and the arts.

Care

Opals are quite delicate and not very hard, so take care not to scratch them.

They are also very porous so they should never be submersed in any liquid. Simply clean them with a soft, damp cloth.

Peridot

Just like diamonds, peridots are formed deep within the earth's fiery mantle below the crust, and they only come to the surface through volcanic activity. Peridots are the earthly twins of moldavite that reach the earth on meteorites.

Another name for peridot is the evening emerald.

Appearance

Peridot is always green but the shade ranges from light, yellowish green to deep olive green, depending on where it was found. The amount of iron in the stone determines its color.

The stones are opaque but after being polished, peridots become clear. They naturally occur either as fine grains or prism-like crystals. The crystals are not rare, but many of them are not of good quality.

Healing Applications

Peridot is nature's tonic that heals tissue and stimulates regeneration. It boosts the metabolic rate while strengthening the heart and lungs.

It helps to alleviate insomnia and ensures restful sleep.

Peridot works with the heart chakra to remove jealousy and anger. The energy soothes and calms the heart and mind and helps us to forgive ourselves.

Care

Peridot can shatter easily and should be handled carefully. Avoid sudden big temperature changes and keep it away from acids and ammonia.

Rinse your stones in running water to clean them and leave them to air-dry.

Pietersite

Pietersite is a striking form of tiger's eye, also called the Tempest Stone because of its swirling colors. It is a member of the quartz family.

It forms in the crevices that are left in jaspers after asbestos disappeared from the jaspers.

Appearance

Found initially in 1962 only in Namibia but later also in China and Madagascar, pietersite is a mottled gray-blue to golden-brown stone. The stones are iridescent and usually small.

Real pietersite has become rare due to small quantities having been found, so counterfeits are frequently offered as the real thing.

Healing Applications

Pietersite can help to balance hormones and the endocrine system to regulate metabolism and blood pressure.

It also boosts digestion for the proper absorption of nutrients.

Pietersite works on the solar plexus and third eye chakras. It activates our personal will to succeed and fires up our drive to make our dreams come true.

The stone can calm emotional turmoil and restore our shaken mental equilibrium.

Care

Although pietersite is a resilient stone being a type of quartz, it is sensitive to some of the acids commonly found in household cleaners, especially sulfuric acid, bleach, and ammonia.

It is one of the few gemstones that can be cleaned in an ultrasonic cleaner. Avoid steam cleaners, however, because the high temperature can cause color changes.

Pyrite

You may know pyrite better as "fool's gold." It got that nickname because of its rich golden color, but the structure and striations are completely different from gold.

Pyrite has a high iron content and when struck with iron or another hard stone, the pyrite produces sparks. Its name comes from the Greek word for 'fire,' which is *pyr*.

Appearance

Pyrite is a gemstone with a brassy color and metallic luster that resembles gold.

It can be found in almost all countries and stones are easily obtainable.

Healing Applications

Pyrite is valued for its protective properties. It not only protects against negative energy but also against environmental toxins. It, therefore, promotes well-being inside and out. Placed in a room or by the door of your house, it can work magic on clearing the energy in the space.

It is a strong meditation aid because it works on the third eye and solar plexus chakras, opening our minds to universal truths.

Pyrite purifies the oxygen we breathe to improve our cardio-vascular functions. It cleanses the body and gives an instant energy boost.

Care

Pyrite does not require special treatment and is easy to clean. Do not, however, store it with other stones because it can get scratched.

Rhodochrosite (The Stone of the Merciful Soul)

The name of this beautiful gemstone comes from the Greek words *rhodon*, meaning 'rose,' and *chros*, meaning 'color.'

The stone is sometimes called Inca rose because large amounts of it were discovered in Inca silver mines that were abandoned in the 13th century.

Rhodochrosite only found its way onto the world markets by 1940.

Appearance

Pink and light red are the most common colors for rhodochrosite, although they have also been found in orange to light brown tones. The stones are banded in a zigzag pattern with white.

Rhodochrosites are mostly opaque and transparent crystals are rare. They are usually found in an aggregate form and single crystals are seldom seen.

The main sources are in Argentina, South Africa, and Colorado in the US.

Healing Applications

Rhodochrosite urges us to open our hearts to change so that we can find what we yearn for. It prepares us for new adventures, but always with compassion and love.

This stone is a gentle reminder to take care of ourselves,

otherwise, we won't have anything to offer to others. It is an excellent guide to releasing trauma and grief and its high energies nudge us back to a state of calm consciousness.

Rhodochrosite is also an excellent meditation companion. It resonates specifically with the solar plexus chakra.

The stone has an overall physically revitalizing effect.

Care

This is a soft stone that will get scratched and chipped quite easily, so take great care with it.

It is soluble in hydrochloric acid, so just wipe your stones with a soft, damp cloth to clean them.

Rhodonite (The Stone of Love)

This rosy pink gemstone is so highly revered that it was designated the national stone of Russia in the 1900s. The Moscow Metro and Mayakovskaya Station boast 80 square meters of columns that are inlaid with rhodonite.

Appearance

The color ranges from a fruity pink to a rosy red. It often has a mottled appearance with flecks of black.

The stone is mostly opaque but rare translucent gem-quality forms have been found.

Besides Russia, rhodonite can be found in Spain, Sweden, Mexico, Germany, and Brazil. It is sometimes also called manganese gravel and fowlerite.

Healing Applications

Rhodonite is the perfect stone to help you leave petty, unimportant issues behind you and see life in perspective. Associated with the heart chakra, it opens us to unconditional love and helps us to notice the small things that are important.

It helps to level our energy levels during the day while staying engaged with our surroundings and experiences.

Rhodonite calms anxiety and comforts us in difficult times. Kept in a living or working space, it can help to restore the equilibrium of anyone moving through it.

The stone is often used to relieve the discomfort of insect bites and it can assist in wound healing to prevent scarring.

Care

Rhodonite is medium hard and can withstand normal handling and cleaning.

Ruby

Red rubies don't need an introduction. With its status of being one of the four precious gemstones besides diamonds, sapphires, and emeralds, rubies have been a favorite of kings and nobles for centuries. In Sanskrit, the language of the ancient Hindus, it was called *Ratnaraj*, meaning "the king of precious stones."

Appearance

The vibrancy in the red color of rubies distinguishes it from the hue of red found in stones like garnets. Unpolished stones are opaque, but they polish to a sparkling brightness.

It is not difficult to get hold of uncut stones, but polished rubies are quite expensive.

Most countries worldwide have deposits of rubies.

Healing Applications

Ruby heals and strengthens the heart chakra as well as the root chakra. It stimulates love and passion, filling us with renewed vigor.

The stone is credited with the ability to gather and focus energy to provide us with a reservoir of life force to be used to accomplish any task we apply ourselves to.

Physically, ruby is used as an excellent aid in detoxification. It stimulates the lymph system to heal infectious diseases and fevers.

Care

Rubies are hard—only diamonds beat them on the Moh

Scale of hardness. They can withstand robust handling and wear.

It is still advisable though to avoid contact with harsh chemicals.

Sapphire (The Stone of Wisdom)

The name sapphire comes from the Greek word for blue and the stone has been used since antiquity as a reminder of the majesty of the heavens. The Greeks made sure they were wearing a sapphire when they visited the Oracle of Delphi to curry favor with the god Apollo.

The clergy wore sapphires during the Middle Ages because they believed it symbolized heaven, while queens wore them to attract wealth and protect them against poisons.

Appearance

Although blue is the best-known color for sapphires, they come in all colors except red. The names of the other color varieties are designated by their color modifiers, for example pink sapphire.

Both sapphires and rubies are varieties of the mineral corundum, which is why there are no red sapphires.

The most expensive sapphires are orange and are known as padparadscha. The name comes from the Sinhalese word for "lotus flower."

Healing Applications

Sapphires are used to improve the elasticity of veins and stem excessive bleeding. It can also help to treat blood disorders.

Because of its blue color, it is associated with the throat chakra and can bring relief from headaches and sore throats.

It is believed that sapphires bestow inspired vision, enhance creativity, and boost concentration. Sapphires can also help us activate our psychic abilities and give us the courage to speak up from our inner wisdom.

The stone is also the friend of lovers, inspiring faithfulness and commitment.

Care

Sapphires are very hard and can withstand normal handling and cleaning. It can be cleaned with a soft brush, in warm, soapy water.

It is also one of the few gemstones that can be cleaned in an ultrasonic cleaner.

* * *

Sardonyx

Archeologists have tracked the use of sardonyx four thousand years back to Egypt. The women wore necklaces with cameos carved to show the goddess of love, Venus, to attract true love.

Soldiers wore amulets and rings with carved images of Mars, the god of war, into battle for protection.

Sardonyx is a type of agate that is often dyed to enhance the colors of the bands in the stone.

Appearance

Sardonyx can appear in a range of colors from dark orange to red to black.

Healing Applications

Sardonyx symbolizes strength and courage, so it is no surprise that its physical healing uses involve the bones and lungs. It also strengthens the immune system and helps the body to absorb nutrients effectively.

The stone pushes us to believe in our potential and to stop at nothing until we reach our goals.

Care

The stone is quite hard, but the surface does show scratches easily. Use only a soft brush to wash your sardonyx and keep it wrapped in a soft cloth when it's dry.

Do not expose sardonyx to a lot of heat or extended periods of direct sunlight.

Scolecite (The Stone of Inner Peace)

The name of this fascinating mineral comes from a Greek word that means 'worm.' The reason behind this is that the stone curls up like a worm when heated with a direct source such as a blowtorch.

The first report of this member of the zeolite mineral family was first reported in 1813 in Germany.

Appearance

The colors range from white, pink, and purple to yellow and red, while some stones are colorless.

The crystal form is rare and can only be found in Iceland and certain parts of India. Other types of mass growths of scolecite occur worldwide.

Healing Applications

As suggested by scolecite's nickname, it brings great inner calm and helps us to relax and unwind. It is a great aid in meditation because it works on the upper chakras.

Used by the bed, it can unlock our third eye for lucid and intense dreaming.

Scolecite is an auric cleanser that pulls negative energy from our minds and bodies. The stone absorbs the energy, so it is important to clean or smudge the scolecite after each use.

Sluggish blood circulation can get a boost from scolecite and digestive issues will be cleared.

. . .

Care

This is a soft and brittle stone, so if you're lucky enough to find one, handle it with care. It is not recommended for use in jewelry because it is so soft.

Water is not a friend of scolecite, so just wipe it with a soft, damp cloth.

* * *

Seraphinite (The Stone of Angel Wings)

The silvery mica inclusions resembling feathers in seraphinite inspired its name. The Seraphim are the highest-ranking angels in the Christian Bible and the feathers reminded scientists of angel wings.

Appearance

The most common color is dark green to grayish green, with the feathery, silver-white streaks looking like highlights against the dark background. It polishes to a magnificent luster and looks truly remarkable.

It is a rare stone and has only been found in Siberia and Australia. If you're looking to purchase one, it will be your best bet to go to a specialist store.

. . .

Healing Applications

Living up to its angelic reputation, seraphinite can help us to connect with the spiritual world and enhance positive energy. It can open our perceptions to understand our souls' counsel, rather than following our hearts or minds.

It is a great tension reliever, but its frequency is high; make sure you are comfortable with such high vibrations, otherwise, you might end up with a headache.

Care

Seraphinite is quite sensitive to pressure, heat, and chemicals. If warm water alone is not enough to clean the stone, you can use a small amount of a mild detergent, but no citrus.

They are sensitive to acids, so avoid having them touch perspiration.

Store your seraphinites on their own in a soft bag.

Sodalite

The first European record we have of sodalite comes from 1811, when mineralogists discovered it in Greenland. Sodalite has, however, since been traced back to the Caral people who lived between 2,600 and 2,000 B.C.E. near Lima.

Sodalite is often mistaken for lapis lazuli.

Appearance

This is a beautiful, deep blue stone, often with white calcite inclusions. The blue can be from dark to light, or even have a violet tint.

It is found in several countries; the prerequisites are a rich alkali environment, but with a low silica content.

Healing Applications

Sodalite is a great tool in a crystal healer's bag. It unlocks our intuition to gain profound insights to overcome daily obstacles.

It is also used as a stone for introspection. Meditating with a sodalite will help you to see yourself as you truly are and evaluate your strengths and weaknesses honestly.

Sodalite balances the metabolism to the optimum rate for you and cleans the lymphatic system. It can also help to reduce fever and bring high blood pressure down.

Care

Sodalite is durable but not hard. It can last for a long time if cared for properly and stored separately.

It is also sensitive to high heat, chemicals, and pressure.

Warm, soapy water and a soft cloth will be enough to keep your sodalites in top condition.

Sugilite

A unique gem, sugilite is only found in South Africa and Japan. It belongs to the mineral class of silicates and was only discovered by a Japanese geologist, Ken-ichi Sugi, in 1944.

There was little excitement about the new mineral at first because the stones were dark brown, and jewelers weren't interested. Everything changed when exciting purple formations were discovered in 1979 in a South African manganese mine.

It is also known as royal lazelle, royal azel, cybelene, and royal lavulite.

Appearance

The stones range from deep purple and violet-pink to lilac. They are usually opaque and subtly banded.

You might need to visit a specialist gem dealer to get hold of sugilite.

Healing Applications

Sugilite is widely recommended as an excellent pain reliever because of its high manganese content.

It is also used to lessen epileptic seizures while soothing the brain and nerves to function in balance again.

It is used as a protective stone against negative energy, and it helps us to release all worries.

Sugilite can open the door for us to forgive ourselves and

others by allowing unconditional love to enter us through the crown chakra and spread right down to the root chakra.

Care

It is a medium hard stone on the Moh Scale, but it is vulnerable to household dust containing quartz. Rather than wiping them with a dry cloth, wash them in soapy water and then dry them with a soft cloth.

Avoid using any chemicals or ultrasonic cleaners.

Sunstone (The Stone of the Warrior)

The legend surrounding the formation of sunstones is that a Native American warrior was wounded by an arrow. His blood dripped on the stones and infused them with his essence, giving the stones sacred power.

It is also known as heliolite.

Appearance

This spectacular variety of feldspar is found in crystallized masses with a sparkly, metallic glitter. The colors are yellow, orange, and red-brown.

The crystals can be either opaque, or clear and transparent.

It is found in Germany, Mexico, Brazil, South Africa, the US (Oregon specifically), Canada, Norway, and Greece.

. . .

Healing Applications

Sunstone is associated with a warrior's heart, full of courage and strength. It stimulates self-healing and harmonizes all our organs.

It lifts depression and replaces it with the radiance of the sun.

Sunstone is primarily associated with the root and sacral chakras. It anchors our self-identity and boosts our benevolent leadership qualities.

Care

Feldspars are vulnerable to heat and chemicals. Warm, soapy water and a soft cloth are all that's needed.

Store them away from harder stones to avoid scratches and nicks.

* * *

Tanzanite (The Stone of Return)

A striking deep blue tanzanite in a lovely pendant.

The sensationally blue-violet stone that was named after its country of origin was only discovered in the 1960s. To this day, tanzanite is only found in a tiny corner in the east African country Tanzania.

It has been predicted that the tanzanite mines will run dry soon, making the gemstone more sought after and sending prices skyrocketing.

Appearance

Tanzanite colors range from light blue to deep sky blue, with red and violet flashes when light reflects from the stone.

The intense violet-blue color that many people may associate with tanzanite is only obtained when the cut stones are heated to 1,022 degrees Fahrenheit.

Healing Applications

Tanzanite is a great stone to use when you need to return to your spiritual roots. It gently nudges our perceptions in the right direction and stimulates intuition.

Despite its high vibrations, tanzanite has a soothing and calming effect because it connects all our components and realigns us, as whole beings, to the universe.

It urges you to be authentic while remaining compassionate. It pushes us to shed our metaphorical skins of complacency and speak constructive words from a balanced throat chakra.

Because of its stimulating effect to the top three chakras, it is also believed that tanzanite can clear throat and mouth infections and relieve headaches.

Care

The intense heat treatment tanzanites undergo to produce the valuable color means that it should never be subjected to sudden temperature changes. The stone may crack.

Light won't affect the color but ultrasonic or steam cleaners might.

The stone is hard when treated properly and won't chip without some very hard knocks, but it can scratch easily.

Turquoise

An excellent example of turquoise, showing the veins clearly.

Most people know the turquoise color as a striking mix between blue and green, but did you know that the gemstone turquoise can also be found in yellow?

The blue-green variety is the best known because of all the archaeological discoveries of carved objects in ancient burial sites. Turquoise was revered as a stone that could bring good fortune and a favorable reception in the afterlife.

It was so popular that the early Egyptian mines in Sinai were already worked out in 2,000 B.C.E. The Egyptians even created a goddess, Hathor, who was known as the Lady of Turquoise.

Turquoise reached Europe through Turkey and that led to the name; the French words for a Turkish stone are *pierre turquois*.

Appearance

The copper deposits in the turquoise create the dark brown and black veins crisscrossing the intense blue and green hues. The stones are opaque and polish to a lovely luster.

Turquoise is easily obtainable but there are many fakes, so be sure to buy from a reputable dealer.

Healing Applications

Crystal healers use turquoise to attract abundance and happiness. It is also used to promote tranquility in your surroundings and bring hope in the hearts of anyone who despairs.

Turquoise is believed to impart protection against injury from accidental falls.

The presence of turquoise stones in your house will ease financial worries and open the door to prosperity by bringing your creative energies in balance again.

Physically speaking, it boosts the immune system, regenerates tissue, and supports the effective absorption of nutrients.

Turquoise is also often used to reduce excess acidity, relieving conditions such as gout and rheumatism. Its anti-inflammatory properties help with detoxification and alleviate muscle cramps.

Care

Turquoise is a soft and porous stone, so care should be taken with it. It should not be immersed in water and avoid bringing any chemicals into contact with it. Oils are also no friend to turquoise.

Store your turquoise stones separately and avoid knocking them against each other or anything else.

Make sure to cover your mouth and nose if you are going to cut any turquoise; the high copper content can harm the respiratory tract if the dust is inhaled.

Unakite (The Stone of Vision)

This colorful piece of rock is credited with having strong enough vibrations to break through any stagnant thoughts and feelings to open our third eye and bring us back to the visionary state we were intended to be in.

The high frequency of unakite's energy comes from the combination of minerals that makes up its composition. Unakite is a type of granite that contains epidote, quartz, and feldspar.

Appearance

The main colors are green and pink, mixed to display a mottled appearance. After polishing, the color patterns are striking and eye-catching.

It is easily accessible and sourced mainly from the US, South Africa, Brazil, and China.

Healing Applications

This is the perfect stone if you are recuperating from a serious illness. It gently supports the body to regain full strength.

Unakite boosts the growth of healthy hair and skin, especially during pregnancy. If you're trying to fall pregnant, unakite can boost ovulation.

Both its main colors work on the heart chakra, so it can help to make our interpersonal interactions authentic and transparent. It also brings spiritual harmony and restarts any stalled mental or emotional development.

It encourages a grateful attitude for everything that happens in our lives, even if there is a hard lesson to be learned from it.

. . .

Care

Unakite is a hard stone that does not need any special treatment, besides being careful around chemicals and bleaches.

Vanadinite

When you look at this vibrantly colored crystal, it is easy to be so dazzled by its beauty that you forget the dangerous elements that formed vanadinite. The stone starts with lead ore that gets corroded in dry climates. The lead is joined by vanadium, and chlorine and oxygen do the rest.

Appearance

The colors range from vibrant red, orange, and yellow, to orange-brown and yellow-brown. The crystals are transparent and usually quite small.

The main source of vanadinite is the US and it might be difficult to get hold of crystals in some countries. There are some deposits in Namibia, Russia, Austria, Morocco, Tunisia, and the UK.

Healing Applications

Vanadinite is a great healing stone for chronic exhaustion. Keeping one next to your bed will make sure your rest is invigorating while making sure your creativity and imagination will be soaring the next day.

This crystal is associated with the lower chakras, and it stimulates your sense of fun and daring.

It is also useful to help us make sense from our physical existence and it grounds and centers us in the earth's energies.

Vanadinite can be a strong ally if you want to manifest something specific, keeping your focus and thoughts on track.

Care

Both vanadium and lead are toxic to humans, especially when breathed in. Do not cut or grind this stone without wearing a mask, and do not immerse it in water to make any elixirs.

The stone is soft and brittle and should be handled carefully to avoid chipping and scratching. A thorough wipe with a soft, damp cloth should be enough to clean your vanadinites.

The Key Takeaways

- The properties of many crystals overlap, although each one has its own exclusive uses too.
- The best way to choose the right crystal is to let your intuition guide you when weighing all the aspects of a particular stone's energy.
- Always make sure about the potential toxicity of the crystals you choose.

Chapter 5

The Crystal–Chakra Relationship

The locations of all the chakras.
"The crystals we are drawn to are more times than not the crystals that we need for healing."

Quote Master, n.d.

Crystals are exceptionally suited to chakra work. Their strong, pure vibrations put them in direct contact with our own energy centers that are grouped into the various chakras.

A Brief History of Chakras

For those of you who are unfamiliar with the chakra system, here is a brief walk through the history of the concept.

It originated during the Vedic era in India that stretched

from 1500 to 500 BCE. Hindu texts from that time talk about *nadis* or energy channels in the body.

The energy hierarchical system was first described in about the eighth century CE, although they only described four chakras at that stage.

The modern word *chakra* is derived from the Sanskrit word *cakra* that means 'wheel' or 'circle.' The image of a wheel of power at the center of an empire can be found throughout Indian literature (Feuerstein, 2003).

What Are Chakras About?

A chakra is a focal point of a specific type of energy in the body. It groups organs and organ systems believed to be associated with that energy type together.

Although 114 chakras are recognized, only seven of them are viewed as the main centers. The chakras are arranged into seven different dimensions, each with 16 aspects.

The chakra system that is known in the West consists of, in ascending order, the root, sacral, solar plexus, heart, throat, third eye, and crown chakras. The top three are in the spiritual realm and the lower three on the physical plane. The heart chakra connects the two parts, forming a bridge between the higher and lower energies.

In the rest of the chapter, we'll look at each chakra in turn, discuss its characteristics, and identify the crystals that work best to balance that chakra.

* * *

The Root Chakra (Muladhara)

The lowest chakra is the root. It is located at the base of the spine, between the genitals and anus. The root chakra represents our survival instinct, our basic desire for security, and our need for self-sufficiency. It is strongly associated with stability on all levels, including the physical.

An open and fully functional root chakra produces feelings of being grounded and stable. This chakra is also important in cultivating self-confidence and a strong, positive self-image.

A blockage or imbalance can result in feelings of mental and physical unsteadiness. It can lead to depression, anxiety, irritability, and a lack of motivation.

Physically, a blockage in the root chakra can manifest itself in problems such as hypertension, impotence, infertility, lower back pain, lethargy, and indigestion.

Crystals for the Root Chakra

The color associated with the root chakra is red, so carnelian, garnet, red jasper, red aventurine, and bloodstone immediately come to mind.

In addition to the red stones, the black stones that assist in grounding and warding off imbalances such as onyx, hematite, black tourmaline, and smoky quartz are also beneficial.

Carnelian

We have already talked at length about carnelian in one of

the previous chapters. Specifically in relation to the root chakra, red carnelian can help alleviate worries about finances and shift a poverty-and-lack mindset.

Garnet

Deep, rich red garnets function at a high vibration level. They boost our survival instincts and give us the courage to make tough decisions when they are needed.

Garnets stimulate energy and promote its free flow through the body to energize all the other chakras in turn.

Red Jasper

The delicately striated red jasper is an excellent grounding stone. When worries about your physical survival threaten to overwhelm you, red jasper can help to keep your feet firmly and courageously on the ground.

The stone has a high iron content, anchoring its vibrations in the earth.

Red Aventurine

This stone can be described as our crystal call to action. It tells our physical bodies how to focus mental energy into action. Red aventurine is a powerful aid in manifesting physical abundance. It also helps to turn a negative money mindset into something positive and effective.

It reawakens our enthusiasm for life and gives us the strength to persevere with confidence.

Bloodstone

Bloodstones in different color combinations.

Bloodstones look almost like a crossover between the red and black stones. It works great to boost confidence and flagging courage due to physical survival issues.

It symbolizes bravery and growth. According to legend, bloodstones originated at the crucifixion of Christ; it is said that his blood fell on the ground and the drops turned into bloodstones (Ancillette, 2022).

Black Onyx

The pitch-black onyx is associated with being grounded, strong, and confident. It helps to draw out negativity and protects against self-limiting beliefs.

Using a black onyx for the root chakra can quickly sharpen your focus so you can see your way out of your troubles, creating a feeling of safety and security.

Hematite

Hematite is a strong grounding stone that helps to restore emotional and mental balance. It also strengthens physical endurance and mental strength.

If a blocked root chakra is causing you to feel negative, hematite can neutralize the negative energy and greatly reduce anxiety.

Hematite also boosts willpower to overcome any harmful indulgences and bad habits.

It boosts clear, logical thinking, making it a strong ally in business matters that are affected by the root chakra.

Black Tourmaline

We have discussed this stone also earlier. It is especially empowering for the root chakra because of its strong protective qualities and the ability to transmute lower energy vibrations.

Smoky Quartz

Smoky quartz grounds and centers. They restore focus and boost physical and mental energy.

It has a strong link with the earth and can dissolve emotional blockages that result from an imbalanced root chakra.

. . .

How to Use the Crystals on the Root Chakra

You can hold a crystal in each hand while doing a healing meditation or lie down for five to 10 minutes with a crystal on your groin area.

You can also place your crystal between the balls of your feet to help center and ground you.

* * *

The Sacral Chakra (Svadhisthana)

The sacral chakra, situated just under the navel, is associated with creativity and sexual expression, as well as living up to your personal potential.

An open and balanced sacral chakra prepares us for taking on new projects, crafts, or life experiences. It brings out our innate desire to be exuberant, spontaneous, and generous.

Blockages and imbalances can show up in a lack of inspiration, mental blocks in creative pursuits, irritability, anxiety, and a diminished desire for sexual intimacy.

On a physical level, it can lead to reproductive issues and infertility. It can also bring on lower back pain, low blood sugar, joint problems, and unrelenting fatigue.

Crystals for the Sacral Chakra

The color of the sacral chakra is orange, so its beneficial crystals and gemstones are also in this vibrant hue.

Orange Carnelian

The orange variety of this stone is very strongly associated with vibrancy, creativity, and a lively spirit.

It can also revive flagging enthusiasm for taking on new challenges and give you the courage to take them on confidently.

Orange Calcite

This is an excellent stone to clear out negative energy and replace it with motivation and creativity.

Orange calcite works gently on the sacral chakra to let go of bad habits, remove apathy, and live to the fullest again.

Tiger's Eye

This lush brown stone can effortlessly rebalance your yin and yang, help to stabilize rollercoaster emotions, and ground you again in your own truth.

Tiger's Eye can also help you to set your personal boundaries without building walls to keep everyone out because you will be secure in your self-confidence.

Amber

Amber is practically brimming over with earth energy, being born from trees. It is fossilized tree resin but is still often used with crystals to heal the sacral chakra.

The fauna and flora contained in its heart carry energies that transcend time. That can help you to reconnect with your intuition and creativity. Your spontaneity, including with sexual matters, will also receive a boost.

Sunstone

Sunstone is the ideal boost for motivation and confidence. It empowers you to take charge of your emotions and relation-ships, but with a light and joyful energy just like the sun.

Goldstone

Often called the stone of ambition, goldstone can free your spiritual power to let your personality shine confidently.

It can help to calm and stabilize emotions, clearing the stage for a sustained focus on creativity.

Aragonite Star Clusters

The peach-colored, delicate crystal clusters resonate with creativity and self-sustainability to bring a renewed sense of balance, both in ourselves and in nature.

It can neutralize the stress, frustration, and anger that so typically build up in a hectic, modern life. The cluster forma-tion radiates energy and is super-grounding.

. . .

Tangerine Quartz

All the versions of quartz are powerful crystals, but the bright tangerine version is specifically suited to balancing the sacral chakra.

It encourages a playful curiosity that brings your *joie de vivre* back and deepens your self-knowledge.

* * *

Solar Plexus Chakra (Manipura)

The third chakra acts as a transition point between simple and complex emotions. It is sometimes called the radiation point of personal power.

It is located over the diaphragm in the upper belly and is the seat of your personal identity, energy, confidence, and freedom. Its associated color is yellow.

When blocked, digestive issues, eating disorders, and diabetes can result in the body. Physical fatigue and allergies also frequently occur.

Psychologically, people with an excessive need for control, a victim mentality, or feelings of insecurity are likely to have problems with their solar plexus chakra.

Crystals for the Solar Plexus Chakra

Any crystal or stone with yellow as the only or predominant

color works with the solar plexus chakra. If you can get out in the sunshine while using your crystals, their effect will be amplified.

Citrine

The bright yellow stone that looks like frozen sunlight aids confidence and the cultivation of a motivated mindset to push through with your goals.

It can also help you to set your personal boundaries and enforce them gently when faced with people that can harm your self-esteem.

Pyrite (Fool's Gold)

Pyrite blocks negative energy. It helps you to stay focused on your goals with a clear mind. It also acts as a protector of your positive mood.

Peridot

Peridot's special type of light green is so close to yellow that the stone can go both ways.

It encourages forgiveness and the release of negative thought patterns so that healing can start. After a peridot cleanse you'll be able to learn the necessary lessons from past experiences and then let them go, focusing on your personal growth.

. . .

Yellow Jasper

Yellow Jasper is a great stone to boost confidence. It can also help the wearer to push through procrastination and finish projects with new energy.

Heliodor

The name of this stone means "gift from the sun" in Greek. It brings the richness of the sun into our thought patterns, bringing a clarity of vision to make difficult decisions.

For those of us who face burnout in our modern hectic lives, heliodor can replenish our mental energy and restore a zest for life.

Golden Healer Quartz

Golden quartz gets its vibrant yellow color from the iron oxide trapped within the stone. That gives it a strong connection to the earth's energy. It is great for opening blocked energy channels, allowing healing on all levels to start.

Yellow Aventurine

The lovely bright yellow aventurine can play an important role in finding balance between your renewed personal power and the amount of control you take. You can almost say it brings a subtle hint of playfulness to leadership.

· · ·

Yellow Fluorite

The near perfection of fluorite's exquisitely ordered internal matrix is perfect to help us calm and order our racing minds.

It can enhance imagination and resourcefulness while strengthening our good intentions.

Golden Mookaite

This unique gemstone is found only on the banks of the Mooka Creek in the Kennedy mountain range of western Australia. That corner of the earth is believed to be strongly connected to the earth's electromagnetic field.

The stone boosts connection between all living beings and renews their confidence in their uniqueness.

Heart Chakra (Anahata)

The heart chakra can be described as the center of the body's energy system. The flow of energy is regulated through the anahata center just like a physical heart controls the flow of blood.

It is in the center of the chest. Its associated color is green, bringing a promise of renewed growth and love. An open and balanced heart chakra opens us up to give unconditional love, closeness, and trust without fearing the potential emotional cost.

If you have any trust issues, whether with other people or merely in trusting your own gut feelings, it is likely that your heart chakra is blocked. Blockages and imbalances can also show themselves in neediness in relationships, or, to the other side, being too distant.

Crystals for the Heart Chakra

The heart chakra's pink and green encompass some of the most beautiful gemstones and crystals in existence.

Rose Quartz

I bet this one didn't surprise you. Roses and pink are virtually synonymous with romantic love. It is the perfect choice to purify and deepen relationships.

It also strengthens empathy with all other beings by replacing all our low, negative vibrations with the higher vibrations of love and acceptance.

Emerald

It's as if the brilliant green color of an emerald calls to you to open your heart and allow love in. Emeralds bring us the gift of a renewed capacity for joy.

Emerald also boosts wisdom in relationships to bring people closer to each other than they ever were.

Green Aventurine

Just like the yellow aventurine, the green version brings a

soft energy that soothes friction while maintaining personal boundaries. In a relationship, that can bring new opportunities for connection.

With green aventurine's help, you'll be better able to discern the things that matter to you and your happiness.

Malachite

Malachite, also called the stone of transformation, helps with the release of the negative energy that blocks the heart chakra. It replaces the negative with a loving and balanced vibration.

Empaths find malachites useful to safeguard them against getting overwhelmed by other people's emotions.

Rhodonite

Rhodonite encourages forgiveness and the willingness to compromise to save and repair relationships. It helps us to transform pain into a positive energy and move forward again.

Green Jade

The green variety of jade is known for setting the imagination free. That brings renewed growth to stagnant relationships, helping them to flourish in unexpected ways.

Amazonite

If you struggle with putting your love into words, amazonite can help. The stone forms a bridge between the heart chakra's feeling of love and the expression thereof from the throat chakra.

Living with a controlling partner can create problems in relationships. With the help of the amazonite vibration, you'll find it easier to set your personal boundaries and express your truths with a loving attitude.

Pink Tourmaline

A great calming aid, pink tourmaline can soften emotional pain, help to release anxiety, and strengthen our intentions to act from pure love.

Chrysoprase

This stone is sometimes called the healer of broken hearts because of its unique ability to equalize turbulent emotional balances. That opens the way to accepting changes without losing your love.

* * *

Throat Chakra (Vishuddha)

Located at the base of the throat, the throat chakra is the seat of genuine and truthful communication. The concept of truth in this context refers to both our personal truths as individuals and our collective truths as humans.

Balancing and opening a blocked throat chakra can heal old childhood traumas stemming from feeling unheard or prevented from getting a chance to speak up for yourself.

Signs of problems in the throat chakra include frequent lying, incessant chatter that doesn't add value to the listeners, insensitive remarks, and social timidity.

In the physical sense, you might experience a chronically sore throat, thyroid issues, jaw pain, unexplained mouth ulcers, and hearing problems.

Crystals for the Throat Chakra

The color of the throat chakra is blue and there are numerous blue and bluish stones that can do wonders for a blocked throat chakra. We'll look at only a few of the more important ones.

Lapis Lazuli

An exquisite lapis lazuli bracelet.

Lapis lazuli was once known as the stone of kings. Its deep and brilliant blue hue assists with the release of anger and helps communicators to be honest in both the spoken and written word.

The stone can ease irritations to clear the mind.

Turquoise

Turquoise is truly the communicator's friend. It can clear old ways of thinking that no longer serve you and prevent you from speaking truthfully.

Aquamarine

An aquamarine can bring hidden emotions into your consciousness, so they can be recognized and dealt with.

People suffering from stage fright often keep a turquoise crystal close to help them overcome it.

Angelite

Angelite tempers the spoken word with compassion and understanding. It can also help to open the channels between people and their angels and guides.

Azurite

Azurite works to resolve stale emotional issues so we can clear out their negative energy and fill our words once more with truth.

The stone should be kept out of direct sunlight and heat because it is soft. The color will fade quickly in the hot sun, while too much heat will turn it completely black.

Blue Lace Agate

There's a soft but powerful energy emanating from the delicate blue lace agate that works gently but effectively on the throat chakra. It helps to neutralize the effects of angry words and encourage us to counter them with divine truths.

Blue Apatite

Blue apatite's deep hue promotes calm communication, without negativity or anger.

It is also a great aid to stimulate our intuition.

Sodalite

Sodalite has a strong vibration that boosts the clear expression of our thoughts. It promotes and strengthens connections and friendships.

* * *

Third Eye Chakra (Ajna/Agya)

We know the sixth chakra as the third eye chakra, but it is also often called the brow chakra, mind chakra, or guru chakra. It is associated with intuition, wisdom, and a profound spiritual awareness.

Most people think the third eye is in the middle of the forehead, but it is a bit lower. It sits right between the eyes, above the bridge of the nose and between the eyebrows.

When in balance, the ajna chakra enhances spiritual abilities, such as clairvoyance, and brings inspired creativity into our lives. It directly influences our circadian rhythms and banishes brain fog.

A blocked third eye chakra causes an intense sense of confusion. It can start with a vague sense of dissatisfaction with life that increases in intensity. Fuzzy thinking will exacerbate the mental unease even further, bringing with it a desire to break free from old patterns. This can lead to depression and anxiety, as well as insomnia.

On the physical side, headaches, vision problems, hearing issues, and imbalanced hormones frequently occur.

Crystals for the Third Eye Chakra

The third eye chakra is associated with bluish purple and deep purple.

Blue Aventurine

If you're looking for a stone to clear out stagnant negative energy so that truth can break through again, blue aventurine will boost your courage to grow spiritually.

As a member of the quartz family, it is abundant all over the world, but that is not the only reason why it is also known as a healer's stone. Some healers work only with aventurine to help their clients overcome addictions and stay strong enough not to fall back.

After the removal of harmful patterns, it is much easier to embrace and voice spiritual truths again. Blue aventurine is beneficial to the throat chakra at the same time as healing the third eye chakra, forming a natural bridge between the two.

Labradorite/Spectrolite

This mineral can often be found carved in the shape of a heart. It is called the stone of magic because of its powerful ability to protect us against negative energies and stimulate deep, meaningful, active connections.

Iolite

Iolite, a variety of cordierite, has a lovely deep indigo blue color. It can balance our male and female energies to free us to concentrate on communication with the divine energy.

It is a powerful stimulant of creativity and can be a productive muse to keep on your desk.

Blue Fluorite

The versatile fluorite can be found in several pastel colors.

The purple variety relates to the third eye chakra. It boosts mental sharpness and refocuses the mind to understand different viewpoints before coming to conclusions.

Pietersite

Pietersite is believed to stimulate the pineal gland. That puts the logical mind temporarily on hold so that our higher consciousness can take over and open our hearts again to understand spiritual truths we may have forgotten.

The stone is a great boost for intuition, and it also stimulates creativity.

Tanzanite

The high and strong vibration of tanzanite is often described as a self-awakening stone. It stimulates deep insight into the universe, breaking open intuitive wisdom to guide you gently back to fulfilling your soul's purpose.

The stone unites the energies of the third eye, throat, and heart chakras to help us function as whole beings that see and speak loving truths.

Crown Chakra (Sahasrara)

The crown chakra is located above the top of the head. It is our connection with the divine.

The crown chakra has been described as an energy sanctuary for the mind that creates renewed intimate awareness of the source of all beings.

Its associated color is violet.

When blocked or out of balance, the whole physical body can feel unstable and uncoordinated. Psychologically, mental confusion and a feeling of disconnectedness can result.

Crystals for the Crown Chakra

The best crystals for working with the crown chakra are violet, purple and white. These are stones that resonate primarily with the higher consciousness.

Amethyst

The richly colored purple amethyst is one of the most spiritual stones in existence. It functions at a high vibration and can calm the mind with an instant connection to the divine.

Amethyst encourages focus and intuition, sweeping away stress and anxiety. It is an excellent companion for meditation.

Sugilite (Lavulite)

This deep purple crystal unites all the chakras down from the crown, bringing with it an understanding of what the spiritual path for your life is. It will help you to reconnect with your purpose and identify the steps needed to realign yourself with it.

Sugilite can also help you to accept life's lessons as stepping stones on your path, not obstacles.

Apophyllite

Apophyllite is also called the stone of truth because it links the physical and spiritual worlds. That, in turn, will help strengthen your confidence in the spiritual wisdom you perceive in yourself.

It can delve very deeply into emotional wounds, so be prepared to face some difficult truths if you want to work with apophyllite.

Howlite

Howlite is a cleansing and aligning stone. It calms the mind and lifts the mood.

It is also effective to absorb anger, replacing it with patience and self-control.

White Calcite

White calcite also clears the aura and renews hope. It banishes stagnant energy and paves the way for new beginnings.

The white crystal with its recognizable 'dog-tooth' shape boosts our motivation to grow and let go of the mistakes made in the past.

. . .

Serpentine

Serpentine is the stone that provides us strength to stand up for our own truths and beliefs, rather than trying to conform to others' expectations.

Its earthing vibrations help to center our scattered minds for deep meditation and introspection.

White Agate

This stone relates to balancing the male and female sides of the personality to release anger, negativity, and frustration.

It also helps to attract spirit helpers and guides.

The Key Takeaways

- The seven main chakras are energetic pathways through our bodies.
- Each chakra is associated with a color and several crystals, among other things.
- The energy channels can get blocked or unbalanced, leading to disease and discomfort.
- Crystals can reopen and balance the affected chakras to restore harmony in our minds, bodies, and souls.

Chapter 6

Crystals in Other Practices

"I didn't choose the crystal life; the crystal life chose me."

Crystal Rx, 2020

Crystals and their energies are versatile and helpful in so many ways. Besides wearing or carrying them around, they can also fit into and enhance any healing, clearing, or balancing routine.

Let's look at some of the modalities where crystals come in handy.

Feng Shui

With the help of the ancient Chinese practice of feng shui, we can create living spaces that are attuned to the flow of life energy, or qi in Chinese. According to old Asian teachings, we need a connection to nature to flourish. When we follow the

153

feng shui principles, we bring that connection into our immediate surroundings.

Being attuned to the movement of qi makes us mindful of our environment. We start noticing small details and can delight in them again, just like when we were children.

When you awaken to the world's magic, you will bloom and live up to your full potential. Does that sound like crystal healing yet? You can bet the same principles are at work here for our highest good.

The core concepts in feng shui are the bagua map and the five elements. Even though there are several different schools of feng shui, all of them use a bagua energy map and the five elements.

The Bagua Energy Map

Although this book is not about the details of feng shui, it is necessary to understand the basic principles to appreciate how crystals can enhance a feng shui practice.

The Chinese word *ba* means 'eight' and *gua* means 'area.' The eight areas in a bagua map represent the areas of energy at work in our lives. Each area also has its own associated element, symbol, color, mineral, crystal, pattern, organ, shape, time of day, and Asian zodiac animal.

The bagua is usually applied to the floorplan of a room, house, or office. It can, however, be adapted to be as big as a city or country, or as small as your hand or face.

In Western style feng shui, the areas in the bagua are:

Wealth	Recognition and Reputation	Love and Marriage
Element: Wood Associated colors: Purple	Element: Fire Associated colors: Red and burgundy	Element: Earth and Fire Associated colors: Pink, orange, red, burgundy, and yellow hues
New Beginnings and Family Element: Wood Associated colors: Blue, teal, and green	**Health and Center** Element: Earth Associated colors: Brown, orange, yellow, and all earthy tones	**Children, Creativity, and Completion** Element: Metal Associated colors: White and gold
Knowledge and Self-Cultivation Element: Earth and Water Associated colors: Cream, beige, taupe, yellow, dark blue, and black	**Career and Life Path** Element: Water Associated colors: Black or any dark color	**Benefactors and Travels** Element: Metal Associated colors: Gray, white, and black

The Five Elements

Feng shui works with the elements of earth, fire, water, wood, and metal.

Each element is related to several deeper aspects and meanings such as colors, seasons, crystals etc.

The earth element is associated with our physical being in all its aspects. This ranges from our bodies and minds to our finances and dwellings. Stones that provide grounding are especially helpful with this element. When the earth element dominates however, you will experience boredom and a heavy, sluggish feeling.

Fire relates to movement. It symbolizes our zest for life and motivations, as well as our physical metabolism. Too much of this will result in frequent anger and impulsive actions.

The water element is all about our emotions, as well as the lymphatic and circulatory systems of our bodies. It is also concerned with our ability to let go of the past and flow toward a new future. If you are feeling a bit overwhelmed by your emotions, you might have too much of the water element in your surroundings.

The element of wood is associated with our flexibility, personal growth, and intuition. Like a tree is always reaching toward the sky, wood enhances our development and creative expansion. Too much earth will bring about stubbornness and stagnation.

Metal is all about logic and clear mental processes. In a room where metal dominates, you will find focused action, analytical thinking, and a high degree of organization. Dominant metal can, however, result in a hypercritical attitude and speaking before thinking.

Feng Shui Uses for Crystals

Besides grounding and protecting us, crystals can also be used to increase financial abundance, create a healthy self-love, boost energy, cultivate passion and inspiration, and deepen our spiritual connections.

Crystals work especially well in the earth areas, grounding and settling a nagging feeling of instability, but any crystal vibrates with enough energy to enhance your whole feng shui practice.

You can choose your crystals according to their colors and their healing properties.

- Wealth area: Amethyst, pyrite, and citrine. If you have any clusters of these stones, this will be the area to put them.
- Recognition and reputation: Carnelian and red jasper, preferably in pyramidic shapes.
- Relationships: Rose quartz, pink opal, pink tourmaline, and morganite. Be sure to use rounded shapes.
- New beginnings and family: Green quartz, jade, green aventurine, and lapis lazuli.
- Health: Tiger's eye, citrine, and agate.
- Children, creativity, and completion: Clear quartz, hematite, and crystal balls.
- Knowledge and self-cultivation: Blue sodalite, blue lace agate, and apatite.
- Career and life path: Black tourmaline, hematite, blue kyanite, black kyanite, and blue calcite. Irregular shapes will work in this area.
- Benefactors and travels: Smoky quartz, moonstone, obsidian, black tourmaline, and any natural stones in circular or oval shapes.

Where to Place Your Crystals
If you are using crystals for grounding, placing them in the

center of a room or home works well. The center of any space is connected to the earth in feng shui.

In a bedroom, keeping crystals on the nightstands or even sleeping with one under your pillow can help you achieve your goal for that area.

If your aim with the crystals is protection, try placing a grid of the right stones such as black obsidian under the four corners of your bed or in the four outside corners of your home.

The front door of a home is extremely important in feng shui. If you want to attract more wealth and abundance, be sure to place one or more crystals at the main entrance of your house or office. This will invite abundance in and welcome it into your life.

Feeling a bit uninspired to get your work done well? Keep a crystal associated with the fire element such as carnelian on your desk.

Good Spots for Specific Crystals

We have touched on the importance of the main entrance or front door of a space in feng shui. It is regarded as the mouth through which all abundance and happiness enter. Placing a citrine (or a couple of them) near the front door will invite all the good energies to join you in your home.

Add some black tourmaline to the citrine at the entrance to ward off any negative energies that might want to accompany your good fortunes. You can also place black tourmaline in all the corners of your house.

The amount of water energy that is present in a bathroom,

especially when the bathroom is an ensuite, can disrupt sleep. Use smoky quartz in the bathroom to calm things down a notch. Its grounding energy will bring balance and stability.

As work companions, pyrite and selenite are great. While the selenite can chase any stagnant energy out, the pyrite can re-energize you. You can put selenite above the doorway with the point toward the exit, if it's a pointed crystal. Pyrite kept under the desk can clear the brain fog caused by electronic equipment away.

Rose quartz and amethyst should be your first choice for the bedroom if you want to give your romantic life a boost. Amethyst brings a tranquil energy that is open to love.

A chunk of clear crystal in the center of your space can help to keep your energy throughout the whole house grounded.

Is your garden struggling a bit? Try placing some green crystals such as aventurine and calcite in several spots. Green stones boost energy and growth.

Reiki

Reiki is a powerful energy healing practice that originated in Japan. Though there are different forms, the best known one is called Usui reiki. The Buddhist monk Mikao Usui discovered reiki in the early 1920s while praying and fasting for 21 days on Mount Kurama. He later explained that the methods of reiki were given to him during one of his prayers. He started teaching others and, according to the inscription on his memorial, he trained more than 2,000 reiki practitioners in his lifetime.

What truly sets reiki apart from other hands-on types of energy healing is Usui's insistence on attunements. This creates a spiritual connection between the reiki student and the universal life force, so that reiki practitioners will always be mindful of the fact that they are not doing the healing; they are only channeling the universal energy. Reiki does not cure diseases, but instead channels enough energy through their hands to the recipient to manage their symptoms, start their innate, natural healing process, and improve general well-being.

The life force is known as *qi*, and reiki creates a flow of *qi* to anyone or anything that is being treated. All of this is natural—we have known about reiki since childhood without realizing it. Remember when you fell and grazed your knee? You immediately ran to your mom to kiss it better—and it helped! That was reiki at work.

Certified reiki practitioners can be at either first, second, or master's level. With each level new skills and symbols are learned and each one requires its own specific attunement before the student is qualified.

A typical reiki session lasts between 15 and 60 minutes and the practitioner remains in a meditative state all the time. The client is likely to experience some warmth and/or tingling in the areas of the body that are receiving the energy. The areas won't necessarily correspond to where the practitioner's hands are because the chakras have wide spheres of influence.

Combining crystals with reiki healing is pushing the effect almost into overdrive because both reiki and crystals work with the purest forms of energy possible. The stones pick up on the intent and energy of the healer and magnify them. While the reiki treatment brings an overall improvement and helps to create an environment for the body in total to heal, the crystals focus the energy on specific organs or issues.

The crystals you want to work with can either be placed on the body or held in the hands; we'll discuss some of the alternatives a bit later.

Good crystals to start with are aquamarine, rose quartz, tourmaline, topaz, amethyst, amazonite, selenite, lapis lazuli, red jasper, sodalite, and moonstone. If you must choose just one crystal that will do the best job in general, you should go for clear quartz. That clears the whole auric field and works on all the chakras in a general sense.

You can choose and group your crystals according to the chakras, or according to the issues you want to treat.

Practical Ways to Use Crystals in Reiki

Crystals should be programmed before the first use in a healing session. This is done by holding the crystal between your palms and activating the reiki energy flow. Hold the purpose you want to use the crystal for in your mind and tell the stone what it is needed for. You will feel warmth emanating from the stone to your hands.

Stay in this position until the warmth cools, which typically takes between five and 15 minutes.

A crystal reiki treatment is divided into clearing and preparation, channeling of the energy, and expressing gratitude.

There are several ways to incorporate crystals into a reiki practice and one of the most powerful is to make a grid.

Using a Grid

It has been said that every crystal on the grid represents power equal to a second or master level reiki practitioner.

The grid should be hexagon-shaped and contain six crystals around the perimeter. Some experts prefer pointed crystals but if you don't have six of those, pebbles will also work. A pyramid crystal should be placed in the center.

Make sure the crystals you are going to work with are clean and charged. Place photographs of the people for whom the reiki is intended or notes with your intention in the grid and send reiki to all the stones for two to three minutes.

Keep the reiki sessions up for twenty-four hours, with intervals of your choice.

Symbols

Symbols are important tools for a reiki practitioner because each one refers to a particular intention. They are known by names such as the cho ku rei/power symbol, the distant healing symbol, the raku/inner peace and freedom symbol, and dia ko myo/deep healing and transformation symbol.

Forming a symbol with an amplifying crystal in the hand will magnify the intention and energy of the symbol. The symbol can be either traced in the air or on a person's body to convey their message.

. . .

Ethereal Crystal Work

For some reiki practitioners, it is also possible to work virtually with crystals. Their crystal attunement sensitizes them for the vibrations of specific crystals, and they can activate the energy by merely thinking about the stone.

This is effective because everything is energy and vibration; although we are used to physical contact to activate a connection, it is not essential.

Tips for Working With Reiki Crystals

- It is always a good idea to start a session with a reiki scan. That will give you an overview of the person's problems and show you which chakras are closed or out of balance. Many people already know which chakras are the problems, but it can never hurt to verify their opinion with your own observations before you choose your crystals for the session.
- Don't use any cracked crystals or stones. That can obstruct or distort the energy. Instead, thank a broken crystal for its loyal service and bury it near a tree to heal itself. If you can't get yourself to separate with a cracked stone, keep it on a place such as a windowsill where it can soak up the sun's healing rays.
- Allow clients to bring their own crystals, if they

have any. If they already have an instinctive connection with a crystal, it will make your work as a reiki practitioner much easier. Their choice of crystals can also provide you with much information about the areas that need healing energy. The spiritual connection with a stone sometimes defies explanations, but the body and mind know what they need.

- If you can, separate your personal crystals and stones from those used on clients in reiki treatments. If you cannot do that, you will have to cleanse and recharge your crystals every time before you use them on yourself. If the healing energy is allowed to continue freely, the power of those crystals will also grow stronger.

Crystals are like an extra set of hands and an extra mind during a reiki session. Use them, they want to help and heal us.

Meditation

The deep state of relaxation and tranquility that can be reached through meditation is surpassed by few other activities. Meditation silences the constant jumbled stream of thoughts to bring about new perspectives, deepened self-awareness, and increased creativity.

Medical conditions brought on or exacerbated by stress can

also be managed and improved by the deep state of calm attained through meditation.

There are various types of meditation and crystals can be incorporated in all of them.

General Pointers for Meditating With Your Crystals

The first step will be to ground yourself and activate the energy of the crystals. Some experts such as the crystal healer and certified meditation leader Carol Boote recommend connecting intuitively to the crystals you want to use and asking their permission to use their energy (Stokes, 2020).

Once the permission is obtained, you can connect to the crystals' vibrations while breathing deeply and keeping an open mind to receive their message.

The crystals should not be kept on the body for longer than 20 minutes per session. If any crystal makes you feel uncomfortable or causes distress of any kind, remove it immediately and drink some water to speed up detoxification.

Because the crystal vibrations are strong, it is not recommended to use them more than once a week. Our bodies and minds need time to assimilate and process the energy that was added to our systems.

A Few Effective Methods

Just as with reiki, building a grid of crystals and stones around you will make their energy available without any stones touching your body. If you are worried about the possible effects of touching the crystals, this might be your way to go. After all, you won't get the full benefit of relaxation and receiving new insights if you're thinking about the crystals against your skin all the time.

A grid can also be built in front of you instead of around you, if you prefer.

For those of us who find a warm bath relaxing, meditating in the hot water with some crystals added or arranged around the bath will have a great strengthening effect. Just make very sure that the crystals you want to add to the water will be able to withstand immersion.

If you are meditating with a specific intention aligned with a chakra in mind, you can add crystals for that chakra to amplify your intention. Placing stones on every chakra will help when doing a general balancing meditation.

The best stones to begin with are clear quartz, rose quartz, selenite, amethyst, black tourmaline, citrine, sodalite, tiger's eye, and garnet.

Another great way to experience the power of crystals is to add a crystal singing bowl to your meditation tools. A clear quartz bowl can connect exquisitely with the quartz-like crystal structures in our bodies to enhance a meditation.

The Key Takeaways

- Crystal energy is powerful in other energy healing modalities too, such as reiki.
- The practice of feng shui also works on the energy

of spaces and objects to create a harmonious living environment.

- Crystals can enhance the existing positive feng shui or bring it into any spaces that are negatively charged.
- The right stone can guide us into deep meditation to reach spiritual insights.

Chapter 7

Frequently Asked Questions

"I can't go out tonight, I have crystals to charge."

Etsy, 2022

As a quick reference guide, I have combined a couple of the most asked questions about crystals and crystal healing in this chapter.

If you feel somewhat overwhelmed, feel free to read them first.

Is Crystal Healing Safe?

Yes, crystal healing is safe for all ages and all mental and physical conditions.

Having said that, it is always important to remember that no energy healing modality can substitute the medical advice given by your doctor or other medical professional. Do not simply discard your prescription medicine or treatments in favor of crystals. Instead, use crystal healing as a complementary treatment to speed up your conventional medical regime.

When you start seeing improvements, you can gradually (and in consultation with your medical professional) taper off your medicines.

Also take care when using crystals around small children. Put small stones into velvet pouches to prevent the children from accidentally swallowing a crystal.

Some stones are also brittle and soft and a child playing with them can damage your crystals beyond repair.

It is also extremely important to take any toxicity in the crystals you work with into account. Wash your hands afterward or purchase only polished stones. Never put any of these crystals into water to make elixirs.

Are Crystals Safe for Pets?

Yes, they are. Take care to avoid a pet swallowing or chewing a crystal.

A good solution to this problem is to stitch a small pouch to the animal's bedding. The crystals can be kept safely in the pouch, and it is easy to clean and swap them around for other stones.

Should the Stones Be Raw or Tumbled?

The tumbling process or any other type of polishing will not change the crystalline structure. Your choice depends on the price, the appearance of the crystals, and practical reasons such as if you will be wearing them against your skin.

If you intend to combine several stones, tumbled ones are stronger than the raw crystals and won't get damaged so easily.

How Often Do I Need to Cleanse My Crystals?

The general rules are to clean them before the first use, as well as after every healing session or exercise.

Stones that are simply placed in a living or working space, or worn on you daily for general protection, will need a good cleaning once a week. If you spend time around negative energy during that week, you will need to clean your crystals immediately afterward to recharge them.

Is It True That Crystals Can Dissolve?

Yes, it is true because not all the stones worked with in crystal healing are rocks in the technical sense. For instance, obsidian is hardened glass and amber is fossilized resin. If you are unsure about the hardness of a crystal, check up on its score on the Moh's Scale of hardness. The ratings on the scale are based on the ability of one mineral to scratch another. The highest rating of 10 is for diamonds, while talc has a rating of 1.

Other crystals such as calcite and selenite are porous and when water or other liquids get inside them, their structure will get pushed apart and they will dissolve.

Does Size Matter?

The basic elements of a crystal's healing energy stay the same, whether you have a crumb or a geode. A large crystal will, however, emit a stronger electromagnetic field. This can make its energy too intense for some people.

If you feel uneasy, scattered mentally, or get sudden headaches or nausea, you should try a smaller version of that crystal.

Some crystals emit stronger vibrations than others, regardless of their size. A small, strong crystal can be more potent than a huge pyramid of a weaker one.

Also keep the function of a crystal in mind. If you want to wear it in your pocket or put it into jewelry, having a large chunk just is not practical.

How Do I Know What to Use Each Crystal For?

The properties of crystals often overlap as well as interact with our own energies. A crystal you might be drawn to intuitively will work on you for a specific purpose, but on someone else it might not have the same effect.

Use the guidelines given in the rest of this book and refine them through your intuition. As your experience with the stones grows, your intuitive knowledge about when to use which ones will also grow.

You can program a crystal with a specific healing intent before using it. It will return to its natural state after a thorough cleansing.

Can I Share Crystals With Someone Else?

Opinions are divided on this question. Some people say the person who handles a stone leaves an energetic imprint on it and only that person should use the stone because it becomes attuned to the person's energy.

If that were the case, it wouldn't be possible to keep crystals in a room that is used by several people to clear the atmosphere of all the negative energy that might be around.

Professional, certified crystal healers also use the same crystals on many different clients, every time with great success.

Always remember that a good cleansing and recharging will remove any residual negativity. While it remains your personal decision whether you allow others to touch your crystals, no energetic signature is irreversible.

How Many Crystals Do I Need?

Now that is a question without a right answer, as there are so many beautiful stones around! Just kidding...

The size of your collection has nothing to do with the effectiveness of your crystal healing work. It is more important to have the right crystals for your needs.

Buying every stone you see could blunt your intuition for their voices because of their numbers. Rather wait until you feel a strong attraction to a new crystal before adding it to your collection.

Chapter 8

Other Books by the author

Here's a list of Emily Oddo books you can find on Amazon:

Yoga for Beginners:
Yoga For Beginners: Your Guide To Master Yoga Poses While Strengthening Your Body, Calming Your Mind And Be Stress Free!

Chakras for Beginners:
Chakras for Beginners: Awaken Your Spiritual Power by Balancing and Healing the 7 Chakras With Self-Healing Techniques

Reiki For Beginners:
Reiki for Beginners: Your Guide to Reiki Healing and Reiki Meditation With Useful Techniques to Increase Your Energy and Cleansing your Aura

Emily Oddo

Third Eye Awakening:
Third Eye Awakening: A Beginner's Guide to Opening Your
Third Eye, Expanding Your Mind's Power, and Increasing Your
Awareness With Practical Guided Meditation

Afterword

"May the quartz be with you."

Artisticlog, 2018

There is deep wisdom in the above humorous quote. We have traveled together on a journey to discover the power of crystals and you are now equipped with all the knowledge you need to harness them.

It is up to you if, and how, you are going to use this positive force. The vibrations are waiting to heal and help us if we accept their help.

Now It's Your Turn...

If the information you read here transformed your life, please leave a positive review on the site where you purchased the book. That will make it easier for others to discover crystal power too.

If you enjoyed reading this book, could you please consider posting a review on the platform?

Posting a review is the best and easiest way to support the work of independent authors like me.

>> Leave a review on Amazon US <<

>> Leave a review on Amazon UK <<

It would mean a lot to me to hear from you.

Emily Oddo

References

Ancillette, M. (2022, January 27). *9 best healing stones & crystals for the root chakra.* Angel Grotto. https://angelgrotto.com/crystals-stones/root-chakra/

Artisticlog. (2018, May 1). *Quotes and pictures.* QUOTES and PICTURES. https://artisticlog.tumblr.com/post/173608840476/may-the-quartz-be-with-you

Askinosie, H. (2020 1). *8 lesser-known ways to use crystals in your everyday routine.* Mindbodygreen. https://www.mindbodygreen.com/0-23590/8-lesserknown-ways-to-use-crystals-in-your-everyday-routine.html

Brown, D. (2018, April 18). *6 steps to use crystals in your daily routine.* Yoga Journal. https://www.yogajournal.com/yoga-101/6-steps-to-use-crystals-in-your-daily-routine/

Chee, C. (2021, November 8). *11 best crystals for the root chakra.* Truly Experiences Blog. https://trulyexperiences.com/blog/crystals-for-root-chakra/

Cho, A. (2019, October 14). *What is feng shui design?* The Spruce. https://www.thespruce.com/what-is-feng-shui-design-1274741

Cho, A. (2021, September 2). *How to use crystals in feng shui for better energy flows.* The Spruce. https://www.thespruce.com/ways-to-use-crystals-for-good-feng-shui-1274644

Clark, D. (2015). *Gem formation: How are gemstones created?* International Gem Society. https://www.gemsociety.org/article/gem-formation/

Crystal Rx. (2020, October 24). *Facebook crystal-rx.com.* Www.facebook.com. https://www.facebook.com/crystalrxpnw/

Crystal Vaults. (2021). *Crystal encyclopedia.* Crystal Vaults. https://www.crystalvaults.com/crystal-guide/

Elliott, H. (2020, May 28). The market for crystals is outshining diamonds in the Covid era. *Bloomberg.com.* https://www.bloomberg.com/news/articles/2020-05-28/no-longer-kooky-crystals-are-outshining-diamonds-in-the-covid-era

Etsy. (2022). *Crystals funny quotes.* Etsy. https://www.etsy.com/market/crystals_funny_quote

Feuerstein, G. (2003). *The deeper dimension of yoga: Theory and practice.* Shambhala.

Grigalunas, R. (2019, July 31). *Quartz crystals used as resonators in electronic circuits.* ES Components. https://www.escomponents.com/blog/2019/7/31/quartz-crystals-used-as-resonators-in-electronic-circuits

Hall, J. (2009). *The crystal bible: Featuring over 200 additional healing stones. Vol. 1.* Godsfield.

Hunt, T. (2018, December 5). *The hippies were right: It's all about vibrations, man!* Scientific American Blog Network. https://blogs.scientificamerican.com/observations/the-hippies-were-right-its-all-about-vibrations-man/

Inspiring Quotes. (2022). *45 famous quotes and sayings about crystals.* Inspiring Quotes. https://www.inspiringquotes.us/topic/4164-crystals/page:2

Jackson, V. (2021, February 2). *How to cleanse and charge your crystals as a beginner.* The Manifestation Collective. https://themanifestationcollective.co/how-cleanse-charge-crystals-beginner/

Keeley, S. (2022, January 21). *Where to place crystals for good feng shui, all year long.* Body and Soul. https://www.bodyandsoul.com.au/mind-body/where-to-place-crystals-for-good-feng-shui-all-year-long/news-story/4f5456afd604184803-da2c054d67e5a6

Lee, A. (2020, April 22). *How to charge your crystals.* C Magazine®. https://magazinec.com/beauty/how-to-charge-your-crystals/

Lewis, M. (n.d.). *Pin by Michelle Lewis on crystals in 2022.* Pinterest. https://za.pinterest.com/pin/277112183308901555/

Matthews, T. (2021, October). *Gemopedia—Gemstone encyclopedia.* Www.gemstones.com. https://www.gemstones.com/gemopedia

McWilliams, S. (n.d.). *HGTV presents the elements of feng shui.* HGTV. https://www.hgtv.com/design/decorating/design-101/the-elements-of-feng-shui

Mitchell, K. N. (2018). *Crystal reiki: A handbook for healing mind, body, and soul.* Sterling Ethos.

My Tunbridge Wells. (2021, April 14). *6 expert tips to help you understand the benefits of healing crystals.* My Tunbridge Wells - Family Events, Classes, Child Friendly Day out and Tunbridge Wells News. https://mytunbridgewells.com/benefits-of-healing-crystals/

Quote Master. (n.d.). *Quotes about crystal healing.* Www.quotemaster.org. https://www.quotemaster.org/Crystal+Healing

Regan, S. (2021, June 15). *How to know if your crystals need charging + 9 potent methods.* Mindbodygreen. https://www.mindbodygreen.com/articles/how-to-charge-crystals

Rekstis, E. (2022, January 21). *Are healing crystals for real? Here's what the science says.* Healthline. https://www.healthline.com/health/healing-crystals-what-they-can-do-and-what-they-cant#science

Remedy Grove. (2018, November 23). *Ten common questions on crystal healing.* RemedyGrove. https://remedygrove.com/bodywork/Ten-Common-Questions-on-Crystal-Healing

Rice, A. (n.d.). *Gemstone toxicity table.* International Gem Society. https://www.gemsociety.org/article/gemstone-toxicity-table/

Salon Privé Magazine. (2021, October 23). *Five simple ways to use crystals in your day-to-day routine.* Salon Privé Magazine. https://www.salonprivemag.com/five-simple-ways-to-use-crystals-in-your-day-to-day-routine/

Schlitz, M. (2005). Meditation, prayer and spiritual healing: The evidence. *The Permanente Journal*, 9(3), 63–66. https://www.ncbi.nlm.nih.gov/pmc/articles/PMC3396089/

Serenity Plus. (2021). *Crystals and the elements.* Www.serenityplus.com.au. https://www.serenityplus.com.au/68-want-to-know-more/157-crystals-and-the-elements

Shine, T. (2018, September 19). *How to cleanse, charge, and activate healing crystals.* Healthline. https://www.healthline.com/health/how-to-cleanse-crystals#visualization

Stokes, V. (2020, November 24). *How to meditate with crystals: Getting started, methods, and types.* Healthline. https://www.healthline.com/health/meditate-with-crystals#:~:text=She%20believes%20that%20crystals%20have

Tiny Rituals. (n.d.). *How crystals are formed.* Tiny Rituals. https://tinyrituals.co/blogs/tiny-rituals/how-crystals-are-formed

Images

Babylass. (2014). A set of jewelry made with polished red carnelian beads. In *Pixabay*. https://pixabay.com/photos/red-carnelian-necklace-bracelet-401997/

Brigitte. (2014). A jade figurine of a bear in an amethyst geode. In *Pixabay*. https://pixabay.com/photos/jade-green-bear-art-amethyst-gem-436085/

FlitsArt. (2018). Amethyst crystals in their natural state. In *Pixabay*. https://pixabay.com/photos/amethyst-amethist-crystal-nature-3537911/

Ford, A. (2019). A beautiful selenite lamp next to a selenite candle holder. In *Pixabay*. https://pixabay.com/photos/selenite-lamps-selenite-candle-holder-4411032/

Grabowska, K. (2020). Assorted crystals and gemstones. In *Pexels*. https://www.pexels.com/photo/set-of-colorful-semi-precious-stones-placed-chaotically-on-gray-tabletop-in-jewelry-store-4040599/

Graves, S. (2017). A striking deep blue tanzanite in a lovely pendant. In *Pixabay*. https://pixabay.com/photos/tanzanite-tanzania-blue-purple-2535680/

Hassan, M. (2020). The locations of all the chakras. In *Pixabay*. https://pixabay.com/vectors/chakra-meditation-aura-energy-5628622/

Kavowo. (2018). A magnificent citrine cluster. In *Pixabay*. https://pixabay.com/photos/citrine-crystal-gemstone-mineral-3201605/

Lima, D. (2021). Beautiful azurite combined with other minerals to create a beautiful composition in nature. In *Unsplash*. https://unsplash.com/photos/qsVdNQubLrQ

Lizarazo, S. (2019). The inclusions in emeralds are usually too small to see with the naked eye. In *Pixabay*. https://pixabay.com/photos/gem-emerald-stones-4014145/

Marsiglia, S. (2020). A beautiful uncut piece of rose quartz. In *Unsplash*. https://unsplash.com/photos/XqK6fVdzAjU

McCormack, A. M. (2016). Black tourmaline in its raw form. In *Pixabay*. https://pixabay.com/photos/black-tourmaline-specimen-stone-1609432/

Ogikubo, M. (2020). A magnificent piece of cavanite. In *Pixabay*. https://pixabay.com/photos/cavansite-natural-background-blue-5361854/

Pasja1000. (2018). An excellent example of turquoise, showing the veins clearly. In *Pixabay*. https://pixabay.com/photos/turquoise-rock-blue-stone-geology-3388145/

Sun Studio Creative. (2021). Crystal face rollers in different styles. In *Unsplash*. https://unsplash.com/photos/bGHZEn8U4fo

Synek, O. (2017). The mesmerizing green swirls of malachite. In *Pixabay*. https://pixabay.com/photos/malachite-precious-stone-2775996/

Tooru. (2016). Bloodstones in different color combinations. In *Pixabay*. https://pixabay.com/photos/natural-natural-stone-stone-1239615/

Van den Bergh, A. (2016). A circular grid of moonstones. In *Pixabay*. https://pixabay.com/photos/moonstone-gemstone-mandala-1447240/

Yeo, J. (2020a). Clear quartz crystals in a natural formation. In *Unsplash*. https://unsplash.com/photos/B50NVoyAqwE

Yeo, J. (2020b). Yellow citrine stones among a few scattered green peridots. In *Unsplash*. https://unsplash.com/photos/ROtpifeuw-E